Costa Rica

∽

Folk Culture, Traditions, and Cuisine

Jack Donnelly

Cover caption: *La Nigüenta* is a folk figurine good luck charm. This statue has her mojo backstopped by two lucky symbols on the base: a horseshoe-13 and a shamrock.

ISBN: 1495930882
ISBN 13: 9781495930881

In memory of

Dr. Robert Kaupp,

a tireless explorer.

Table of Contents

Preface vii

Introduction ix

Costa Rican Folk Culture 1

Agüizotes 3

La Nigüenta 7

The Dance of the Little Mare 11

La Pica de Leña 17

The Game of the Little Devils 21

Folk Legends 25

Holy Crocodile! 35

National Traditions 37

Bar Food 55

Bar Soup 69

Fiesta Food 73

Jack Donnelly

Traditional Tico Cuisine   81

Glossary of Food Terms   93

Bibliography   99

Preface

The origins of this book go back to the 1960s in Mexico. I was studying cultural anthropology at the *Universidad de las Américas* in Mexico City. I often took short trips on weekends or during breaks to different parts of the country to investigate interesting cultural practices. Some of these trips provided me material for academic papers. I was able to continue my exploration as a Peace Corps volunteer in Guatemala. I worked with Mayan co-operatives in the Western Highlands and my job entailed a great deal of travel around the area.

I spent many years in ever-so-Anglo New Hampshire, but worked hard to maintain my Spanish (years ago that meant listening to short wave radio). I also maintained my interest in Latin American folk culture with the help of annual visits to my friend Dr. Robert Kaupp of Washington, DC, to whom this book is dedicated. Robert called himself an Ethno-Historian, a fancy term for a real-life Indiana Jones (no whip, but plenty of snakes). He spent the last 20 years of his life searching for Vilcabamba, the lost city of the Incas. A few days listening to his latest adventures in Peru would give me the fix I needed to fuel my hopes of getting back into the field.

Eventually, I retired and chose to move to Costa Rica where I am a Resident Retiree (legal resident, but still a US citizen). I came with hopes of learning all I could about the country, but did not think of writing about it until Mr. Terry Renfer asked me to write an article for the magazine of the Association of Residents of Costa Rica (ARCR). As soon as he broached the topic with me, the proverbial light bulb went on in my head. I owe him a debt of gratitude for that offhand suggestion. Research and writing on this topic have become my geezer avocation.

My research methodology is multimodal, to say the least. I am always on the lookout for relevant books. I scour the Internet for academic papers and articles, mostly in Spanish. I read *La Nación*, the excellent Costa Rican daily, and clip articles on any topic that might prove to be of current or future interest. These articles have proved very helpful in pointing my research in new directions. Finally, there is the arduous task of checking my information through fieldwork; even academic articles sometimes contain egregious errors. This entails traveling to different parts of the country, especially when there is a folk event taking place. I talk to anybody who doesn't hit me with a stick; you never know when a priceless piece of information is going to surface. During these trips, I also have to suffer through eating delicious traditional dishes and talking to the locals about them. It's a tough job, but somebody has to do it.

I need to thank the many Costa Ricans whom I have accosted with endless questions. I am especially grateful to my good friends at Hotel-Soda Las Flores in Heredia: Miguel, Georgina, Gabriela, Mao, Laura, Meli, and all the rest who have taken the time to clarify things for me.

I would like to thank Dr. Jayne Alexander, my proofreader and editorial consultant. She has provided invaluable insight and advice over the years. This work would be far less literate without her input.

Finally, I want to thank the late Mr. Carmine Palleschi. He was my high school Spanish teacher and deserves great credit for his rigorous approach to language instruction. He really opened the door to Latin America for me.

Introduction

The goal of this book is to fill a gap in the English-language literature about Costa Rica. I am trying to illuminate at least a portion of the traditional folk culture of the country. I also identify and describe many of the national traditions and Costa Rican cuisine. In doing so, I hope to dispel the common belief that Costa Rica doesn't have a vibrant folk culture or tasty different dishes worthy of trying. This is a great country to travel around for many reasons, including the folk culture and cuisine. To my mind, travel should involve learning about the customs of the area and trying new and exciting dishes.

The target audience is anybody with an interest in the country, especially foreign residents and tourists who may wish to know a little more about the culture and food. Generally, travel guides give these topics light treatment or leave them out entirely.

Most of the book was written as stand alone articles, some of which have been published in different versions. The book is intended to be read that way, rather than from start to finish. A person planning to go to Guanacaste can turn to the relevant chapters for information about folk events in that province. Another person wishing to try the food in some local pubs can open the book to that section and proceed to chow down. Given this approach, I have kept the MLA format for each chapter as if it were independent (e.g. the first use of a foreign word is italicized, but subsequent uses appear in the normal font). For clarity, there is a small amount of duplication in a few chapters.

The Spanish terms are Costa Rican and often differ from the Spanish of other countries. All translations of content are mine. The term *Tico* is used as a noun or an adjective for Costa Rican.

My goal is to provide the interested resident or traveler with a little more information than they probably need. If they develop a real interest in a particular fiesta or dish, they can review the details and be on their way to a greater level of understanding. I also include Costa Rican Spanish terminology for events and food. I have tried to construct the book in such a way as to allow readers to skip over detail or Spanish they may not be interested in, without interrupting the flow of the text.

Some readers may take exception to my division of folk culture and national traditions. I will readily admit that the line is sometimes fuzzy. Purists (like me) will generally identify folk culture as being local and oral, without any media involvement.

I should apologize to lovers of sweets for the lack of coverage of desserts. I simply do not have a sweet tooth. In fact, Costa Rica has many fine dessert dishes. The glossary was a challenge in terms of what to include and what to exclude. I hope I struck a reasonable balance.

I wish I could say this is the end-all and be-all book on these aspects of Costa Rican culture. I have not covered every fiesta or event in the country. Some, I simply haven't gotten around to attending. Often there are conflicts with multiple events taking place at the same time in different parts of the country. Also, I have tried to be entirely positive in my approach to this work. I have left out some events I have found to be overly commercial or loud and celebrations that might be a little on the rowdy or dangerous side.

Costa Rican Folk Culture

I first came to Costa Rica in the summer of 1969 (gasp!). I had just completed my undergraduate degree in Mexico and I was enjoying a window of time before I had to deal with the Selective Service. The plan was to travel by bus as far south as my money would take me (Bolivia, as it turned out).

My field of study had been cultural anthropology and I had done some field work in rural areas, so I was interested in learning about the practices of indigenous peoples and peasant populations in each country I visited. When I asked about native populations here, I was told something along the lines of, "There were only six of them here when the Spanish arrived and they didn't like the way the neighborhood was going, so they moved to France". Well, that may be hyperbole, but the message was clear: no Mesoamericans here in Costa Rica, just us Europeans.

I had no way of knowing it at the time, but that was my first encounter with what Costa Rican historians call The White Legend: the belief that Costa Rica is (and should continue to be) White and European. The institutionalized denial inherent in this myth even formed the basis for important government policies. The legend is alive and well today, although weakened by better information and assertive minorities.

One unfortunate result of this ideology has been the consistent discounting of rich oral traditions. Traditional Tico practices originated from many sources including Europe, but also Amerindian cultures; Spanish Colonial heritage; African-Caribbean influences; and Asian immigrant culture. Many people would add the United States and modern Latin America to this list. Once adopted, they evolved, blended, and became entirely Costa Rican.

Costa Rica is well known for its eco-tourism, sandy beaches, surfing, adventure activities, bird watching and lovely climate. It's time to jettison The White Legend and adopt an appreciation of the full cultural landscape: Costa Rica has its own rich mosaic of folk culture.

Agüizotes

Agüizotes are the folk beliefs, small superstitions or minor *brujería* (witchcraft) of Costa Rica. Dionisio Cabal Antillón, the noted cultural journalist, calls them the magical roots of Costa Rica[1]. They encompass all aspects of life: love, death, birth, luck and the small daily annoyances that plague us all. One saying goes, "*Para la suerte y la muerte, no hay escape*" (For luck and death, there is no escape). Escape may be well beyond our mortal powers, but it is altogether human to try to bend luck in our favor.

For those empiricists who refuse to believe in anything beyond the world they feel to be scientifically validated, the appropriate Tico saying is, "*No hay que creer, ni dejar de creer*" (It is not necessary to believe or disbelieve).

We North Americans are certainly no strangers to a raft of similar personal sorcery. We knock on wood for luck or to ward off some expectation of malevolence. We throw salt over our shoulder (right hand, left shoulder) after a spill. I know many rational educated people who went to great trouble to bury a statue of St. Joseph, upside down, in order to conjure up a buyer for their house. Even the most modern of skyscrapers gets an evergreen tree to top off the highest structural member, as an entreaty to the Pagan powers that be to grant luck for the building.

We also have many ethnic and regional beliefs. In the South, the New Year is started with a meal of black eyed peas, greens, and pork. On this day, lobsters are bad mojo because they move backwards, while pigs root forward. A main course of winged fowl is also mangled magic as it could allow the luck to fly away.

The greens, the color of money, are an entreaty for financial success for the year to come.

The agüizotes of Costa Rica vary widely by region, ethnic group, age, and even by family. The newspaper *La Nación* did supermarket interviews about them one December and found a wide variety of family New Year practices involving food, herbs, and spices.

There are countless Costa Rican agüizotes and few Costa Ricans would be familiar with all of them. Many are practiced with several variations. Here are some examples:

Knock on Wood – This is attributed, in both cultures, to the Christian cross, made of wood. It likely goes much further back to the animistic belief of spirits residing in trees. If you are really serious about it, you will knock three times (Trinity?). Interestingly, in Spanish you will also say, "*Machalá*", an Arabic word meaning, "*Dios no lo quiera*" (God forbid). There are many such words in Spanish left over from the almost 800 years that the *Moros*, Berbers from Northern Africa, occupied at least some part of Spain.

Scissors or a Blade – At one point, I realized I had brought more knives than I needed for my culinary pursuits. I tried to give one to some close friends who ordinarily love all things kitchen. However, they refused it, explaining that sharp gifts "*Se corta la amistad*" (cut the friendship). They finally accepted it on long-term loan, mine to reclaim whenever I wish. It is also bad luck to leave scissors open.

Love – Any magic worth the name must have the power to call up love. There are a number of spells for this, but a love potion can easily be concocted by boiling the undergarments of the suitor. The resulting liquor is slipped into a beverage and given to the object of their desire.

More Love - One story tells of a smitten young lady hiring a *bruja* (witch) to enchant her intended. The old woman watches her bathe, dress, and apply her makeup. When asked for the spell, the witch replies, "You are the magic".

Unwelcome Guests – To cut short a bothersome visit, simply place a broom, upside down, behind the door.

Dancing with Priests – An unmarried woman who dances with a priest will remain single to dress the saints.

Noxious Animals – Poisonous snakes will be calm and cooperative in the presence of a pregnant woman. Spiders are good luck and should not be killed. Rub your hands in your armpits and you can safely remove a wasp nest.

Animal Omens:

- If a rooster crows at midnight, someone is going to die.
- If a grasshopper comes into the house, you will have good luck. However, if you throw it out or kill it, you are pushing the good luck away.
- If a hen crows like a rooster, it is a messenger of bad fortune. You must wring its neck or cut off its head immediately.
- If a bird in flight defecates on a person, it means good luck. There is no need to clean it off.
- When the household dog lies on its back with all four paws up, the owner is going to get sick.

New Year Charms:

- This is to ensure that food not be lacking in the coming year. On December 31st you should cut open a loaf of bread; stuff it with beans, rice, sugar, cinnamon and a pinch of salt; tie it with a red ribbon or string; and hang it in the corner of the kitchen.
- On New Year's Eve you should ask thirteen people for a coin of the same denomination. This brings good luck.
- To realize a desired trip in the coming year you should pack your suitcase with personal items and carry it around the block at midnight on the 31st.
- On the 31st or the 1st, collect a bouquet of *Santa Lucia* flowers (a small purple flower that grows at altitude). This ensures work in the year to come.
- For good luck, on New Year's Day you should wear something yellow. Some people consider underwear the more potent charm.

This may not be a topic that everybody will be comfortable talking about. Nobody wants to be seen as superstitious, much less a communicant of the dark arts. Gently ask any Costa Ricans you might know what they do in the way of New Year traditions. Try explaining to them your lucky shamrock key chain, that Saint Christopher medal in your car, and the Kitchen Witch over the sink.

[1] Dionisio Cabal Antillón. *LOS AGÜIZOTES Raíces mágicas de Costarrica*. San José, Costa Rica: Cultura Producciones, 2009. Title.

La Nigüenta

La Nigüenta is an unusual ceramic or plaster figurine and folk icon that is completely unknown outside of Costa Rica. It may well have originated with a French curio, but that remains uncertain. It portrays a young naked girl sitting with one leg on her knee picking parasites out of her toes. The noxious creature in question is a *Nigua*, hence the name la Nigüenta.

Niguas are parasitic arthropods called chigoe fleas or jiggers (*T. penetrans*) in English. They are the smallest of the fleas. They should not be confused with chiggers, larval mites found in more temperate climates. The female burrows head-first into the host, leaving the rear of her abdomen protruding through the skin. Infections are almost always on and between the toes. Niguas were a very common pest in Costa Rica when many rural people walked around barefoot. The skin reaction can range from mild irritation to serious inflammation.

La Nigüenta was traditionally used as a powerful all-purpose *agüizote* or good luck charm. Many households had reverent spaces set up for a statuette. Money and other offerings were left by her to ask for good fortune or a particular favor. Today, she is seen as primarily an enchantment to bring economic prosperity. I recently gave two Tica friends small Nigüentas. They were delighted and quickly installed them in their homes. However, when I ran into them a week or so later, both had moved their figurines to their businesses to foster better returns. A Nigüenta received as a gift is considered much more potent that one purchased.

The adoration of this sort of female figure is very Marianist, akin to worshipping the Virgin Mary. La Nigüenta has long been considered a substitute for Mary in Costa Rican folk practice. Marianism is very strong in many parts of Latin America, especially *la Virgen de Guadalupe* in Mexico, the earliest of the great Latin American Virgins. She is also venerated in parts of Guanacaste. Costa Rica has its own *Virgen de los Ángeles* or *la Negrita*. She is the *"patrona de Costa Rica y protectora de las Américas"* (Patroness of Costa Rica and Protector of the Americas).

Interestingly, the Spanish term *Marianismo* is also used by Latin American sociologists to represent the idealized female counterpart to *Machismo*. The wife of the *machista* is expected to be demure and chaste, except for child bearing with her husband. The male is held to no such standard.

How this figure came to represent good luck is anybody's guess. I can't see how the child with the parasitic infestation is all that fortunate. And, it certainly cannot bode well for the fleas she is attacking with her nails. One of the joys of folklore is that you simply have to take it as it is and run with it.

The practice of owning, displaying and propitiating la Nigüenta is a folkway that is dying out. A friend of mine in her early 60s tells me that when she was a child in Puriscal, every house had a Nigüenta. Today, most young urban Ticos will be familiar with her, but are unlikely to have one in their homes. However, she is not entirely lost to the younger generation. You can get a colorful full-sleeve tattoo of her in some San José parlors. She also appears in some modern artwork and the names of Tico blogs.

La Nigüenta is uniquely and quintessentially Costa Rican. It would be a terrible shame to lose such an enigmatic and intriguing Tico cultural motif or to condemn her to the arcane preserve of the artsy elite. She is a wonderful quirky folkloric image in our all too *McModern* world.

Finding an attractive Nigüenta is hard today. You can find cheap, and unattractive, models in tourist souvenir shops, often in two or three sizes. Trust me, asking for one in a store selling religious items will get you a look that says, "We aren't Pagans here!" I am told that small ceramic shops will cast and custom paint one for you. You can find a good selection of different sizes, shades, and styles in the San José central market.

The Dance of the Little Mare

On December 12th of every year, a centuries-old folkloric celebration of *la Virgen de Guadalupe* and *la Yegüita* (the Little Mare) takes place in Nicoya, Guanacaste. This festival marks the culmination of a long, complex, and highly structured community effort. This year-long process is supervised by a religious brotherhood, *la Cofradía de Nuestra Señorita La Virgen de Guadalupe*.

La Yegüita comes from a Chorotega Indian legend about twin brothers. On December 12th in 1653, the brothers were celebrating la Virgen de Guadalupe and had consumed an ample amount of *chicha* (corn beer). Both brothers were in love with the same woman, Nantiume. They began to fight over her with machetes. Terrified neighbors implored la Virgen de Guadalupe to intervene and save them. Suddenly, a small black mare came out of nowhere. Kicking and biting, she got between the combatants and separated them. This was seen by the Chorotegas as divine intervention by la Virgen and has been celebrated ever since.

Today it is commemorated and celebrated with *la Danza de la Yegüita*. In the dance, la Yegüita (a carved wood and fabric costume with a braided tail) dances in quick swirling steps with *la Muñeca* (a small dressed doll on a stick), who represents a Chorotega woman calling to la Yegüita with her movements. The dark color of the doll and the mare is seen as an indigenous attribute. The dance takes place in advance of la Virgen as she makes her way around town and, briefly, in the *Iglesia Nueva* (New Church) at the end of a special Mass on the 12th.

La Virgen de Guadalupe is the earliest and best known of the great Latin American Virgins. She appeared in Mexico in 1531, just ten years after the conquest of the Aztec Empire by Hernán Cortés. She made herself known to Juan Diego Cuauhtlatoatzin, a recent convert to Catholicism, in Tepayac, near Mexico City. Fortuitously, this was a place venerated by the Aztecs as a place holy to Tonantzin (aka Coatlicue), a mother diety.

Her indigenous features and that she appeared to an Amerindian were very important to the relationship between the Spanish and native Mesoamerican population. She became a uniting cultural and racial force in the move toward a greater *Mestizo* culture. She is widely venerated today, both in Mexico and other countries, even in the U.S.

All aspects of the festival are organized and overseen by the cofriadía. It is religious organization dedicated to putting on the event in strict accordance with indigenous tradition and Nicoyan customs as handed down over generations. The organization of this brotherhood is very complex and involves many members, *cofrades*.

Members hold a meeting called *La Elección* on the evening of the 12th. Only women over the age of fifteen are allowed to vote, although both men and women can be elected to the various offices. These offices include *Mayordomo, Nacume* (Chorotega - Boss), *Prioste Mayor* (Head Steward), *Jefa de Cocina* (Head Cook), and others. Each office carries very specific duties that lead up to the successful orchestration of *las Festividades*. These people serve a term of one year, one cycle. The transfer of office takes place on December 13th.

The activities, including fund raising, go on all year long, However, the real action starts each year on November 1st with the *Contadera de Días* (Counting of the Days), an organizational meeting of the officers to start the countdown to the *Gran Celebro* on December 12th.

This is also when they set the date for *la Pica de Leña* (Cutting of Firewood), customarily the second Saturday in November, but never later than the 14th of November. All food prepared during the fiesta is cooked with wood and the Pica is a significant event in its own right. The fuel is transported in *carretas* drawn by oxen. The Pica has a considerable reputation for the consumption of alcohol. The local joke is that la Yegüita has worms and needs to be dosed with *carbolina* (a pesticide). In fact, carbolina is code for *guaro* (booze) which is consumed by the human participants. Locals will also tell you the carbolina sometimes causes la Yegüita to dance right off the street, but parasites are rarely a problem.

There are a number of other important dates leading up to the celebro:

December 8 – *La Entrada de los Empleados*: the real work of food preparation begins in *la casa de la cofradía*.

December 9th – *La Atolada*: preparation of corn, especially *maíz pujagua* (purple corn), roasting cacao, grinding sweetener, etc.

December 10th – *Alza de la Ramada*: Erecting the wood and thatch shed roof on the side of la casa de la cofradía. Donations are accepted under this shelter and drinks are passed out through the side window.

December 11th – *Las Vísperas del Cerebro*: The Eve of the Fiesta. This is when the real public part of the event begins.

The 11th starts out around 4 AM with la Alborada (Dawn) at the Iglesia Colonial with *bombetas* (aerial bombs) fired out of *morteros* (mortars). This operation is handled by a cofrade during the entire festival. Whenever an activity begins, the bombetas herald the location. As la Virgen moves around town, the mortars follow her and accentuate her route and destination. You don't need an app to gauge her location.

La Alborada then moves to a house owned or rented by the *Patrón de Alborada* (Sponsor of the Dawn) where people are provided food, drink and music. Naturally, the bombetas continue.

At noon, la Virgen begins to parade around town, although she is not yet dressed in her best. On the 11th she is attired more simply. There are a number of stops and events during the day, capped off by the singing of the *Salve Regina Mater* at the Cofradía at 5 PM. Later there is a Mass, music and fireworks at the Iglesia Nueva. As she moves around town, la Danza de la Yegüita is periodically performed in the street ahead of her.

December 12th – This is the high point of the fiesta, el gran día de Nuestra Señorita Virgen de Guadalupe. It is the culmination of a year of work on the part of the cofardía.

Again, the day starts at dawn, this time it is called *el Alba* (Dawn). A different Patrón provides food, drink and music. The morteros are hard at work.

At 10 AM there is a Mass, a two hour Mass. The Bishop of Tilarán officiates backed by at least a dozen priests. The Iglesia

Nueva is packed. There is a brief appearance of la Yegüita and la Muñeca near the end of the ceremony after which the procession heads out of the church and down to the cofradía. La Virgen is now ornately adorned and ready for her big day. She travels all around town during the day, but you can always follow the bombetas to find her.

The provision of free food and drink is an integral part of the Fiesta. There are two drinks that are very typical of the day.

Chicheme – A sweetened corn beer, like chicha, but made with the colorful maíz pujagua. As one celebrant, quite in his cups, lamented to me, *"no es muy chichada"* (it's not very beery, no kick).

Tiste – A sweet drink of ground cacao with ginger, but not fermented.

You will be offered both of these elixirs at the Cofradía in traditional *jícaras* or *guacales* (gourds), something my urban Tico friends find amusingly quaint.

The various patrones take charge of a number of activities of the event. They are not officials of the cofradía. Rather, they take their charges on, and this can be quite costly, in fulfillment of a *promesa* to la Virgen. They must be selected and approved by the cofradía and, if there are more qualified applicants than open positions, they are chosen by lottery. I am told that this is often the case.

This fiesta, with its fusion, or syncretism, of Catholicism and Chorotega beliefs, is a tradition that has been maintained for hundreds of years. It is very much a part of the cultural identity of Nicoya, Guanacaste. The residents are very proud of their *Guanacastequidad*, their *Guanacasticity*. The *Nicoyanos* and the cofradía have every right to be proud of the roles they play in bringing to life this impressive religious and cultural event each year.

La Pica De Leña

La Pica de Leña, the cutting of the firewood, is part of the year-long calendar of tasks of the Cofradía de Nuestra Señorita Virgen de Guadalupe (a religious brotherhood) in Nicoya, Guanacaste. The culmination of the work of the cofradía is the annual celebration of the Virgin of Guadalupe on December 12th. The Dance of the Little Mare, *la Danza de la Yegüita*, is an integral part of this event.

La Yegüita comes from a Chorotega Indian legend about twin brothers. On December 12th in 1653, the brothers were celebrating la Virgen de Guadalupe and had consumed an ample amount of *chicha* (corn beer). Both brothers were in love with the same woman, Nantiume. They began to fight over her with machetes. Terrified neighbors implored the Virgin of Guadalupe to intervene and save them. Suddenly, a small black mare came out of nowhere. Kicking and biting, she got between the combatants and separated them. This was seen by the Chorotegas as divine intervention by the Virgin and has been commemorated ever since.

Maintaining Chorotega tradition in every way is central to the ethic of the cofradía and the celebration. The firewood cut on this day is used to prepare the food for the big event in December. In point of fact, the wood is stored for a year to dry. The wood hauled to the cofradía by oxcarts on this day was cut the previous year and stored to dry.

The Pica is scheduled, approximately, for the second Saturday in November, never later than the 14th. It follows closely on the heels of the *la Contadera de Días* (The Counting of Days) held on November 1st. The Contadera is an organizational meeting of the officers of the cofradía to make sure everybody is clear on their duties leading up to the big celebration. The counting of the days and duties is done with different-colored kernels of corn, which are then given as a reminder to the people holding specific offices.

The cofradía comes to life on the Friday before the Pica. Members are busy collecting donations of food and working in the kitchen. It's not open to the public, but the bustle is readily visible through the windows. Trucks come and go delivering meat, corn, and other foodstuffs. There are a few *bombetas* (aerial bombs fired out of mortars), but nothing like the barrage that marks the festival on December 12th.

The Pica is well known as a heavy drinking event. The local joke says that the Little Mare has worms and must be dosed with *carbolina*, a traditional pesticide. Carbolina is simply code for the alcohol consumed by the two-legged participants. Loudspeaker trucks are busy on Friday promoting the various dances and drinking events that mark the weekend.

At 4 AM there are some loud bombetas near the cofradía, signaling the start of the Pica. The regular wood cutters, a weathered rustic group, are fed first with a hearty bowl of *pozol*, a stew made with corn. A long line of younger people, many with beer still in hand, form a line outside and are let in to eat as space allows. Soon the more serious choppers, axes and machetes in hand, head out to a ranch just south of town to start the real work of the day: dropping trees and bucking them up into woodstove length pieces.

Many hands, and a few nontraditional chainsaws, make quick work of the task. The new wood is stored, and wood from the previous year is loaded into colorfully painted traditional oxcarts for the trip into town. By late morning, the parade is well under way. Folk dancers and school bands lead off, followed by a long line of oxcarts. Teams of oxen come from all over Costa Rica to participate. The 40 or so oxcarts are followed by a traditional *tope*, horse parade. Gauancaste is *sabanero* (cowboy) country and there is no shortage of riders eager to prance their mounts down the street. Many people keep and train Costa Rican Fine Step horses just for these events.

The slowest step in the process is the unloading of firewood from the carts into the wood bin at the cofradía. The carts have to back up to the building one at a time and there is only room for a couple of people to throw in the wood. Also, by this time the carbolina is taking its toll on the workers. It's prudent to stand well back from the flying pieces of firewood. The oxcarts and their drivers stand in line for several hours, blocking traffic in that part of town.

At this time, in front of the cofradía, there is also what can only be called an axe dance. Dancers twirl around each other with sharp axes, sometimes interlocking the heads to spin each other around. Others just hold the axes high in the air as they twirl. The dance doesn't last long, but it makes a lasting impression.

The carreta is a national symbol of Costa Rica. Technically, it is the national symbol of work, representing the diligence, sacrifice and work ethic of Costa Ricans. However, it has come to be seen as a symbol of all aspects of traditional Costa Rican life. It has solid wheels to avoid collecting mud between the spokes. In the early 1900s, people started to paint colorful geometric patterns and animals on the wheels and sides of the cart. This decoration is uniquely Costa Rican.

There are many celebrations that feature the carts and the *boyeros*, the ox drivers. This is a particularly good place to get a close look at these wonderful rolling pieces of art. The Pica certainly draws spectators, but the people lining the streets are not as numerous as in many other festivals featuring the ox teams. It is mostly a local crowd and you are free to walk along with the carts, talk to the drivers, take pictures (the drivers will stop for a pose), and inspect the carts and the teams.

The Pica is not an event aimed at drawing or entertaining tourists. It is essentially a step in getting ready for the Virgin of Guadalupe celebration on December 12th. The carbolina and the food are motivating and make the very real work of cutting firewood less onerous. Unless you are interested in all-night drinking and loud music, the parade is the big draw. The activity at the ranch in the morning is also interesting. Of course everybody is welcome to help with the wood.

The Game of the Little Devils

The Brunka are an indigenous people living in the Province of Puntarenas in the south-pacific zone of Costa Rica. Most of the tribe lives in the Reserva Indígena Boruca, in the reserve of Térraba, or in the neighboring reserve of Curré Rey. The Brunka are a Talamancan tribe whose ancestors ruled most of Costa Rica's Pacific coast from what is now Quepos to the Panamanian border, including the Osa Peninsula. They are sometime mistakenly referred to as Borucans, after the name of the large indigenous reserve.

The tribe is best known for the annual performance of *el Juego de los Diablitos* (The Game of the Little Devils) celebrated in Boruca from December 30th through January 2nd and early in February in Curré, known locally as Yimba. This game or enactment reflects the history and cultural lore of the struggles between the tribe and the Spanish conquistadors. However, it remains highly symbolic to the modern Brunka in terms of preserving their culture against the pressures of the outside world.

While people take the symbolism of this event seriously, it is also an occasion of great merriment. A great deal of *chicha* (corn beer) is consumed, as well as large quantities of commercial brew. Despite the alcohol intake, everything is very amicable and jovial. There is laughter, joking, horse play, and nobody takes anything too seriously. Even tourists with cameras fixed in front of their faces are welcomed with smiles and kidding all around. One gentleman, with a few beers under his belt, even offered to sell me his wife, who was well ahead of him in her intake. He assured me that she would not be expensive to maintain. She was oblivious, but he and I had a good chuckle over it. I thought it was funnier once I was certain he was kidding.

The game has more structure than is apparent to the casual observer. There are ten distinct acts or stages and nine separate roles, some with multiple players (e.g. diablitos). The acts and the order of appearance of the characters follow a logical sequence from the birth to the victory celebration.

The story begins with the poignant *la Nasencia* (local dialect for *nacimiento*, birth), which occurs at midnight of the first day on a nearby hilltop. Here, the diablitos are born and this represents the origin of the Brunka people and culture. The devils are heavily costumed with vegetation, burlap, and the wonderful hand carved Brunka masks. These beautiful and exotic masks come in many different shapes and sizes. Some are painted or adorned with fiber hair. They are made locally of cedar or balsa and their sale is an important source of income for village craftsmen.

At dawn the next day *el Toro* appears. Cattle were brought to the New World by the Spanish and the bull represents the invading *españoles*, Spanish conquistadors. He arrives with great fury and begins to throw himself at the diablitos at every opportunity. This battle, *la Lucha*, goes on for three days. The costume is a heavy wooden frame covered with burlap with a carved bull's head on the front. When he charges and hits the diablitos, it is a very forceful blow and they are often knocked to the ground, sometimes more than one of them at a time. There is some effort made not to trample the tourists, but a bull's gotta do what a bull's gotta do, so it's important to stay alert.

Late on the third day a comic figure called *el Carnicero* (the Butcher) appears. His role is to sell the "meat" of the bull. He insists on a minimum purchase of at least one ton and makes a great show of typing up the orders on an old junk typewriter that hasn't made a mark on paper in decades.

On this last day of the battle, the plot takes a number of twists and turns. First, in *la Tumbazón* (defeat), the bull kills all of the diablitos. A Brunka sorceress then brings them back to life. At this point, the bull flees and hides. He is sought after and found by the dogs, played by some of the same people playing diablitos. Then, in *la Matazón* (slaughter), he is killed, with the fatal thrust coming from *el Matador*. This is a great triumph and joyous celebration ensues.

This last stage of the game carries over into the evening. There is a large fire in the field next to the community center and the burlap costume of the bull is ignited. The bull runs around in the darkness wildly streaming flames. He seems to enjoy making a couple runs directly at and through the crowd of spectators and photographers. Make certain you have the footing and the space to get out of his way. Eventually, the bull is fully engulfed in fire and has to shed his costume. It gets tossed onto the fire and he is done for the year.

The game is closely supervised to make sure that everything transpires according to tradition and the fun doesn't get out of hand. The *Diablitos Mayores* (devil elders) and *los Arreadores* (herders) oversee the proceedings and are quick to step in if there is a problem. Once I saw a huge San José bound bus stop for people in the road. A group of about 15 diablitos, fueled by chicha and carried away with the excitement of the game, decided that it would be grand fun to "capture" the bus. It was a little like the old saw asking what a dog would do with a car if he caught it: They could only sort of hug the front of the bus. However, before the driver ceased to be amused by this masked and wildly-costumed whooping mob groping his vehicle, the arreadores stepped in and moved the group on to the next battlefield. The bus then went on its way with many smiling passengers who could truthfully tell the tale of being attacked by a horde of wild natives.

The game can get very rough, or at least seem that way. There was a contingent of Red Cross medics standing by with two ambulances. I asked their supervisor how many diablitos ended up being transported to the hospital from their clashes with the bull. He assured me that it was nowhere near as dangerous as it seemed. He compared it to the *lucha libre* wrestling matches: seemingly violent, but really quite safe. The participants have been practicing since childhood and know how to avoid injury.

At the end of the festivities there is loud music, beer, food and dancing in the community center. People are tired, but happy that another performance of the game has been successful. And, everybody knows the diablitos will be born again next year.

Folk Legends

This is a small sampling of the many folk legends found in Costa Rica. Many are shared with other Latin American countries, especially Central America and Mexico. They vary widely from country to country and even within Costa Rica. You may even encounter multiple versions within the same family. There are many excellent books with these legends, some even illustrated. They are quite comprehensive, but all in Spanish.

EL CADEJOS

The legend of *el Cadejos* is widespread in Central America, Mexico, and there are variations in South America. El Cadejos is a large demon-like dog with fiery red eyes, jaguar teeth, and a huge furry tail. He may sport either canine paws or the hooves of a goat. He drags around heavy thick chains, sometimes unseen, but always heard. In some countries there are both black and white versions of the beast, representing good and evil, or male and female. Costa Rica only has the black, and mostly benevolent, variety.

His function is to follow people, mostly men, late at night when they are out drinking and living dissolute lives. During these travels they are under his protection and no misfortune will befall them. If faced with an attack, Cadejos vanishes and reappears behind any threat to his charge. Also, he enjoys invulnerability to earthly weapons. Clearly, he is a guardian nobody wants to tangle with.

A secondary function, the first in some versions, is to terrify the wayward partier into a more socially acceptable and sober lifestyle. Some local stories tell of whole gangs of male carousers swearing off *guaro* (booze) and turning their lives around with their families and communities. Years later, in hushed frightened tones, they explain that their transformations were a result of an encounter with el Cadejos.

In his spare time, he may also frighten the odd disobedient child into better behavior by appearing in the child's dreams. This seems to be a minor sideline.

The origin of el Cadejos is as varied as his characterization. There may be some ancient basis in the Christian concept of the Guardian Angel or the pre-Columbian belief in an animal counterpart for every human. The name may come from the Spanish word for chain (*cadena*). Some accounts say el Cadejos was a priest who fell short of the mark in caring for his parish and, as penance, was condemned to 100 years in this devilish form. Nearing the completion of his sentence, he tried to end his pain by throwing himself into the crater of Poás Volcano, but merely earned a more permanent curse.

Others say the legend originated with the father of a son named Joaquín or José Joaquín, who cursed the drunken lifestyle of his offspring so vehemently that he, the father, was transformed into a phantom canine.

Another popular version, probably from Guanacaste, relates that the son of a besotted and foul-tempered man tried to frighten his father into better behavior by dressing up in an old fur and rattling chains as the old boozer stumbled home from the cantina. This primitive attempt at an intervention caused the sot such a start that he passed out and fell to the ground. Fearing he had killed him, the son revealed himself and was cursed into an eternal spectral existence by his unforgiving dad.

Interestingly, some literary critics have suggested that el Cadejos was the inspiration for *The Hound of the Baskervilles* by Sir Arthur Conan Doyle. While there are parallels, there are also some English legends that run along the same vein (e.g. the Yeth Hound) and Doyle himself credited these as his inspiration. Ironically, at the end of this story, Sherlock Holmes actually refers to Costa Rica in his explanation of the plot to murder and usurp the property of Henry Baskerville. Holmes describes Beryl Stapleton, the wife of the villain masquerading as his sister, as, "a Costa Rican beauty".

LA SEGUA

Infidelity, generally male, is treated much more harshly in Costa Rican folk legends than late-night tippling. While the hooch-swilling wastrel may suffer a frightening encounter with a demonic canine, the philanderer runs the risk of meeting a femme fatale equine specter that will be the end of him. *La Segua* (also *cegua*, *seguanaba*) manifests as a lovely young lady who transforms into a fearsome apparition intent on extracting heinous female revenge for male unfaithfulness. This is not exactly what the amorous gentleman has in mind.

An unfaithful man in Cost Rica is called a *picaflor* (hummingbird, going from flower to flower); a *mujeriego* (womanizer); a *zaguate* (dog, hound). A less direct way of calling a man a dog, unfaithful, is to say he walks on all fours (*anda de cuatro patas*).

La Segua appears as a lovely young woman to straying men late at night in remote locations. Traditionally, she tempted men on horseback, asking demurely for a ride to a nearby village. More recently, she is said to have modernized her seductive entreaty to include motorized vehicles: changing with the times. Some versions say there is safety in numbers because she will only appear to solitary travelers. Others say she will tantalize a small group of men with the intent of splitting off a lone victim.

Once on the horse or in the vehicle and traveling forward, she transforms into a horrible beast with the head of a mare's skull covered with rotting flesh. Her eyes are great glowing red orbs and her breath has a strong smell of putrefaction. At this point, the terrified horse takes off at a gallop. There is no indication she has the same effect on fuel injection.

The male then suffers tragic consequences. Characteristically, she bites him on the cheek, leaving a large mark with her huge teeth. He may be killed by her on the spot, or die of fright shortly thereafter. If he survives, he will most certainly be insane and live a zombie-like existence. He will die muttering the words, "*La vi, la vi*" (I saw her, I saw her). Some kinder versions of the tale allow a few to escape her wrath. These seem to be men with poorly formed evil intentions or devout relatives, usually a mother, praying for them diligently.

Some assert she is a witch, betrayed by her man, seeking vengeance against all men with faithless hearts. She made a pact with the dark powers that allows her to vomit up her soul into a gourd and make the transformation into the fiend.

She is a common subject for Costa Rican masks. Look for the long horse face at festivals featuring costumed clowns on stilts or masked performers of any kind.

EL PADRE SIN CABEZA

El Padre sin Cabeza or the priest with no head is another beloved Costa Rican tale. It is a frightening story about a traveler, usually late at night and often after a few drinks, who encounters a small church in the gloom. Commonly, this church had not been there before dark and is shrouded in fog. The penitent soul enters the sanctuary in search of spiritual support. There is a service that ends with the celebrant turning around to reveal his headless condition.

The good father does nothing to directly harm the communicant, but the sight of the headless body is damaging enough. The poor soul flees the ethereal chapel in complete panic. The terrified mortal returns home in shock, unable to function or communicate effectively for several weeks. Unlike encounters with other ghostly beings (e.g. la Segua), the victims do recover. Often, they turn their lives around, renounce excessive drinking and carousing, and dedicate themselves to living upstanding lives. Sometimes the lesson extends even further and people are forever afraid to even carry illicit liquor past the site of the phantom church.

Many versions give no background about the cleric's condition; he is simply an apparition of great horror for the living. Other variations tell of a parish priest who struggles with the temptations of the flesh and is repeatedly reprimanded by the bishop for his actions. He tries to walk the straight and narrow, but ultimately becomes captivated by a beautiful parishioner. His downfall is the result of her jealous husband returning home to find him ministering to his wife. Ignoring the cassock, he swiftly beheads the priest and flees town with his spouse.

While this takes the poor padre out of the reach of his unhappy bishop, he is then condemned to an everlasting unearthly, not to mention headless, existence. His ministry is transformed to summoning late-night wanderers with church bells to an eerie Eucharist that will change their lives forever.

An interesting parallel to this legend is his secular cousin, also headless (*el primo del padre sin cabeza*). He is an ordinary Joe who goes about his business as best he can. He does sometimes startle people, although much less so than his ordained relative. People are accustomed to him stopping into the cantina for a few beers and setting his head on the bar.

There is also a story about a headless pirate. However, that seems to be simply an occupational hazard, unrelated to the padre or his cousin.

There is a belief that the headless condition alludes to the practice of the Inquisition to behead witches, heretics, sorcerers, and other offenders. In most versions, it is unclear what offence warranted the decapitation.

LA CARRETA SIN BUEYES

The *Carreta Sin Buyes* tells of a ghostly oxcart that moves on its own through the night, wagon tongue high in the air, as if supported by the yoke of an invisible team of oxen. It moves noisily over the town cobblestones or rough country roads. Often, people will hear the carreta pass by, but avoid the fright of looking out to see it. It is also commonly thought that there is an unseen driver: a witch or even the Devil himself. The cargo box may hold a cadaver or the spirit of a person cursed for bad behavior in life.

The carreta is said to favor neighborhoods where young people are living dissolute lives or where couples are constantly fighting. It may also frequent houses of avaricious people, living or recently deceased.

The legend of how the cart without oxen came to be varies greatly, even by the standards of other local legends. The common theme is that it is scary to those seeing the unnatural vehicle moving through the night without any apparent means of propulsion.

The most common version involves a witch, generally from Escazú (Itzkatzú of old), who used her powers to secure the love of a handsome young man. Years of cohabitation with such a dark force took their toll on him. As he was dying, he begged his love to take him to the church for absolution or last rites. She loaded him into the cart and headed into town. The parish priest would have nothing to do with her devilry and forbade her entrance to the sanctuary. Despite the adamant refusal of the curate, she tried to drive the cart up the steps and over to the altar. He ordered them to stop in the name of God and the oxen obeyed. They were spared the pastor's curse, but the cart, perhaps with the witch and her beloved, were condemned to forever wander through the darkness. Sometimes the witch and her spouse expire together and are brought to the church by a hunchback servant.

Some more complicated versions revolve around the cholera epidemic of 1856. An oxcart may have been used to remove the bodies of victims. More interestingly, a cart is said to have been used by a neighborhood committee to remove potentially dangerous waste from village cesspools. In this version, the men of the Cubillo family, a father and three strapping sons, are charged with the removal of the toxic waste. They work diligently to cart the stuff off in barrels for disposal, under cover of darkness to avoid the stigma of the task. Strangely, during this time it became common for chickens, corn or even pigs to vanish overnight. Even more dramatically, a number of virtuous young village women became pregnant. The more religious members of the community attributed these events to the Holy Spirit. Subsequently, late-night revelers were struck dumb, even blind. Upon recovery, they told a tale of a horrible spectral ox-less cart.

Another common version, also from Escazú, involves the theft of a load of consecrated lumber designated for the construction of a church in San José. The thief used the lumber to build a house, a sugar cane press, a barn, and an oxcart. The thief soon died, but his body was condemned to wander inside the cart.

A simpler and more rural version of the tale involves a cruel ox driver who worked his animals mercilessly. He overloaded the cart and beat the poor creatures when they could not haul the load through muddy roads. Eventually, they expired from the mistreatment. The driver then made a pact with the Devil, exchanging his soul for the eternal satanic propulsion of cart. After he died and the Horned One collected on the deal, it seems the force moving the cart remained. Perhaps Old Nick simply forgot to take off the curse: his line of work does keep him very busy. Anyway, the cart continues to clatter along back roads with no discernible purpose other than to frighten any late-night travelers with the bad luck to encounter it.

LA LLORONA

La Llorona, The Weeping Woman, is a popular legend extending throughout Central America, Mexico and even into the southwest

U.S. It is especially strong in Mexico. It tells of a woman who throws her unwanted child into the river. She then repents her infanticide, but is then condemned to wander the river banks, crying out in search of her child.

The most common Costa Rican version involves a virtuous country girl who is tempted by the material delights of San José. An unprincipled young man takes his carnal delight with her and she becomes pregnant. Unable to face her family or village, she gives birth in secret and tosses the infant into the river.

An indigenous version tells of a chief's daughter, betrothed as a child to a noble of another tribe, who falls for a handsome Spaniard. She also has a child and loves the man and the child with all her heart. On learning of the child, her father throws his grandson into the river and attacks her lover. She is driven mad with grief and flees to begin her life of nocturnal wailing.

Yet another adaptation relates that la Llorona began as a devout Catholic abstaining from relations with her fiancée until they could get a priest to visit their remote village to marry them. She is trapped by a storm with a handsome traveler who threatens suicide if she does not give in to his sinful demands. Her resolve weakens and the story proceeds along the same lines.

This story is often told as a cautionary tale for young people. It emphasizes that they have duties and responsibilities during adolescence and that errors can result in lifelong regrets.

An analogous tale often in conjunction with la Llorona in Costa Rica is *La Tule Vieja (La Tulevieja)* which means the old woman with a hat (or the old hat, but everybody knows what it means). She is another good girl led astray to unwed motherhood. The most explicit version has her refusing to feed her child until it dies of starvation. Subsequently, her breasts swell up with milk and leak continuously. This causes her to be pursued by noxious black flies. She obtains a *tule*, a kind of hat, to protect herself from the pests and it becomes her trademark.

Both legends stress an important tenet of Costa Rican culture: bad motherhood is a mortal offense.

Holy Crocodile!

One of the stranger folk traditions in Costa Rica is practiced in the Guanacaste town of Ortega de Santa Cruz. In this remote village in the northwestern part of the country, there is a group of men called the *Lagarteros de Ortega* or Lizard Men of Ortega. On Good Friday (Holy Friday), they jump into the crocodile infested Tempisque River, armed with only sticks and ropes to capture the largest "lizard" they can find. This has been their tradition for hundreds of years.

The trailhead is a few miles outside of town and is the scene of a festive Good Friday party. There is music, food, a few professional photographers, maybe even a TV video crew, and a lot of people waiting anxiously for the reptilian nightmare to make its appearance. The *Ley Seca*, a ban on alcohol sales for Holy Thursday and Good Friday, is openly ignored.

Many people will hike, ride ATVs, or drive 4 x 4s a mile or so to the river in hopes of seeing the actual capture. They are all carrying heavy coolers, and it's not a very good trail. In fact, the lagateros will not settle for just any wimpy little croc; they want a big one. To accomplish this, they will search until they find a toothy beast worthy of the honor. This may or may not be in sight of the eager onlookers. Either way, the captured critter is carried on their shoulders to a waiting truck at the trailhead and escorted into town by hundreds of spectators.

The hapless croc spends the day as the unenthusiastic guest of honor at the town festival. It is released the following day. Some stories relate that originally the guest was killed on Easter Sunday and its fat used for making curative potions. This minor witch-craft is no longer practiced, but the people of Ortega are fiercely proud of their tradition.

In my experience, the locals can get a little short when asked about the meaning of this tradition. I'm not sure if they are just tired of the question, or if they feel visitors suspect them of something pagan or primitive. They get a determined look on their faces and resolutely state, "It's just our tradition."

National Traditions

Costa Rica is rich in national traditions. I use this term to describe events that are much wider in scope than what some purists (including myself) call folk culture. These traditions enjoy a larger audience and may enjoy the benefit of some government sponsorship. Some are covered by the media. Whatever you choose to call them, they are colorful and interesting.

TOPES

A *tope* is a traditional horse parade. As many riders and their mounts as can be found will parade through town, strutting their stuff for the appreciative crowd. These events are emblematic of the rich ranching heritage of the country. Ranching traditions and lore are especially strong in the northwest province of Guanacaste.

The verb *topar* in Spanish means to bump; *toparse con* means to bump into (somebody). Readers familiar with Mexican Spanish will recognize tope to mean a speed bump, those jarring speed reducers in the road that will destroy your vehicle if you go over them too fast. Here they are called *muertos*, dead bodies, as in a dead policeman in the road. In days of old, livestock came and went through the ports. They made the journey between the ports and the ranches over rough roads in drives. They were, if you will, bumped along the road by cowboys, *sabaneros* in Costa Rica. Thus, the term tope came to be used for a horse parade. Many fiestas and even religious events will feature a tope as part of the festivities.

The annual *Tope Nacional*, held in San José on December 26th attracts around 5000 riders, although the number is always iffy because many of them try to avoid the entrance fee by jumping into line along the way. These riders, both men and women, range from urban sophisticates on costly horses groomed to the max to hardscrabble cowboys on scruffy working mounts. Cans of beer are standard issue, although the city has clamped down on alcohol consumption after some history of riders veering off into the crowd.

The Tope Nacional is a big family event. People stake out space early to be sure of having a good view. Folding chairs, coolers, cameras, along with plenty of beer and liquor, are the norm. Horsemen will often stop for photographs, even hoisting kids up into the saddle for a memorable shot. Vendors hawk inexpensive chairs, big hats, and food. There is considerable police presence, and they keep a pretty tight lid on any trouble makers.

One sure crowd pleaser at all topes is the Costa Rican Step Horse. These animals are rigorously trained to dance or high step their way along the parade routes. They are very impressive to watch.

CABALGATAS

While a tope is a horse parade strictly for show, following an established route through a populated area for the benefit of the spectators, a *cabalgata* is a recreational ride from one place to another. It is more for the enjoyment of the riders than any observers. Many places have these rides as annual events. Sometimes there is an entrance fee that raises money for some worthy cause.

One very interesting cabalgata takes place on the night of the full moon in March. The troop leaves the town of Tempate de Santa Cruz in Guanacaste and goes through the hills to Playa Potrero on the coast. The ride takes about two hours and they split up as they get to Potrero, some going directly to the big party and others circling around to make their approach along the beach. A small musical group in a 4 x 4 truck makes the journey with them. For the sake of tradition, the riders also drive a bull or steer. The animal had big horns; it was dark; I did not think a closer inspection would be prudent.

This ride draws around 400 riders. A big party at a restaurant awaits the riders at the end of the trail. After the merriment, the more affluent riders load up their mounts and leave by truck. Some sad looking souls have to ride back the same dark trail to Tempate, after having consumed an ample amount of beer.

TOROS – COSTA RICAN STYLE

As a young man studying in Mexico, I became a great fan of traditional bull fights. Many years later, I attended one in Spain and found that I had developed too much empathy for the bull to enjoy the spectacle. This is not a problem with Tico style *toros*. Here the bulls are well cared for and almost never injured. Tico friends of mine joke that the bulls' contracts call for air conditioned stalls and conjugal visits.

On the other hand, the human beings get the stuffing knocked out of them. Some editorials even call for the practice to be banned because of the high medical costs incurred in taking care of the battered humans. There is a required insurance policy to be paid for by the organizers, but this statute is often ignored.

Costa Rica has a national health system that ends up treating the all-too-willing victims.

The basic plan for the toros here is to introduce a hostile bull into the ring. To ensure some real snorting taurine ferocity, the bull is given a few jolts with a cattle prod just prior to release. The bull is joined by a large crowd of *improvisados*, improvised bull fighters, essentially anybody who can convince the organizers of their sanity and sobriety (I'm not convinced the exam is all that rigorous). The goal is to get as near to the creature as possible, even better to touch it, without getting gored or trampled. Some people succeed on both fronts, others not so much.

Broken humans are the order of the day, but deaths are uncommon. One Gringo vacationing in Guanacaste decided to give it a try last year and barely survived a horn through the chest. He underwent hours of emergency surgery and spent weeks in recovery. Some of the improvisados dress up for the occasion – Batman, clowns, fuzzy colored wigs, etc. There are a few professionals in the ring who help the injured hobble out. If they need to be carried out, there is an express medical window on the side of the ring. The stretcher can be passed directly into the medical support area. Bulls can achieve great fame by dint of their ferocity; killing somebody is a real career boost.

The big toro event of the year is called Zapote, after the district of San José where the ring is located. It begins on the 25th of December and it runs to the 6th of January, Three Kings Day. There are afternoon and evening events, and they are all broadcast on national TV. For a fee, you can have a personal message stream across the screen below the action. The ring is surrounded with food vendors of all sorts, and it's a great place to forage for fiesta food.

One of the parts of the toros I enjoy is watching the highly skilled horsemen rope the bulls when it's time for them to exit. They take great pleasure in showing off their skill with a lasso. The ropes are often light in color and can be seen very clearly, especially in smaller bull rings.

OXCARTS

The *carreta* or oxcart is the national symbol of Costa Rican labor, but to many Ticos it is the symbol of everything traditional in Costa Rica. As declared by President Óscar Arias in 1988, it symbolizes the culture, peace, and work ethic of Costa Ricans. While oxcarts are to be found throughout Central America, the Costa Rican cart stands out for being painted with colorful geometric designs. This was the idea of an Italian immigrant in the early 1900s. He saw the solid wheels as an endless supply of revolving canvases begging vibrant expression.

The cart is utilitarian in design, nothing Cinderella would consider ball transportation. It is a short, high-sided, two-wheeled wooden conveyance with large solid wheels to avoid the problem of mud accumulation inherent with spokes. It evolved from a Spanish artillery carriage, the *cureña*. There is no seat for riders. The ox driver walks alongside leaving the entire cart for cargo. It is said the scarcity of indigenous labor in the country contributed to the importance of the cart in agriculture. Some other Latin American countries relied more heavily on humans for moving cargo over rough terrain.

The owners of the carts travel to many events and parades around the country. People never seem to tire of the lumbering oxen pulling the colorful carts. The second Sunday in March is the National Day of the Ox Driver, and there is a big parade in Escazú. Late in November there is a big oxcart parade in San José where the carts bring local saints into town. If you want to see the carts performing genuine work, *La Pica de Leña* in Nicoya in the first part of November is the place to go. That is when the firewood is cut for the Virgin of Guadalupe festival in December. Roughly 40 carts haul the fuel into town in a colorful parade.

THE VIRGIN OF LOS ANGELES

According to the legend, on August 2nd of 1636, a young girl named Juana Periera found a stature of the Virgin Mary on a rock in the middle of the forest in Cartago. She took it to the local priest and he put it in a box. The next day he opened the box to inspect it and found it was gone. Juana returned to the place she had found it and discovered it had returned.

This small stone icon became known as Nuestra Señora de los Ángeles, Patroness of Costa Rica and Protector of the Americas. She is more commonly known as *La Negrita*, the little dark one, for her size and color. She spends most of the year in a shrine inside the basilica in Cartago. People travel from all over to pray to her, often covering the last leg of the journey, the length of the church, on their knees.

However, in August her schedule becomes a little more interesting. On the 1st of August she gets new clothes in a ceremony called *la vistación*, the dressing. This is in preparation for August 2nd, her big day. On this day, many thousands of *romeros*, pilgrims, descend on Cartago. The term romero comes from pilgrims traveling to Rome, and by extension to any other religious destination.

The number of romeros is a matter of dispute. The municipality of Cartago likes to throw around numbers like 2 or 2 ½ million. The University of Costa Rica did a study and came up with 770,000; about 16% of the population of the country; enough people to fill the national soccer stadium 22 times. Some of the discrepancy may stem from whether the numbers reflect the entire year or just August 2nd. Either way, a huge number of people make this pilgrimage, called a *romería*.

People walk to Cartago, mostly from San José, about 14 miles away. Some walk from distant parts of the country and start their journey days in advance to arrive on the 2nd. Some roads are closed to vehicular traffic. There are vast numbers of police and first responders assigned to assist the faithful. Every available bus and train is pressed into service to transport people back to San José.

La Negrita gets out of the basilica and there is a procession through town. She travels to the Cathedral of Santiago Apóstal (Saint James the Apostle) and stays there for 30 days. Her return trip in September is another, albeit lower key, event. The return is called *la pasada*.

Unless you are devout and don't mind large crowds, I would point out that this event can be viewed on TV. No matter what the true number of romeros is, it's an awful lot of people all going to the same place at the same time. The basilica is intersting and well worth a visit, during a quieter time. La Negrita is small and hard to see, so you may have to ask to have her pointed out to you.

MASCARADAS

The *mascarada* (masquerade) is a solid tradition in Costa Rica. Performers, including professionals, dress in costumes and masks for many types of occasions. The *gigantes* or *payasos* (giants or clowns) are tall figures with a frame topped with a mask that sits on the performer's shoulders. A hole in the front of the costume allows for breathing and vision. The arms are weighted so they fly around as the character dances and twirls.

In 1996, the Government declared October 31st as the Day of the Traditional Costa Rican Mascarada. This was an effort to reinforce the traditions of mask performance and mask making in the country. The date was chosen to fall on Halloween and just before Mexico's Day of the Dead. In fact, local observances of the mascarada tradition vary a little. Some are the weekend before or after the 31st. The Sunday masquerade event at the Museum of Popular Culture is ideal for families.

Traditionally, the masks represented many characters from Costa Rican legends (*el Cadejos, la Segua,* etc.). Of late, the representations have become more modern. There is also an active debate over the merits of masks made with the traditional paper mache versus fiberglass. The paper mache is much more time consuming, given the need for each layer to dry before the application of the next.

You can see mascaradas at almost any fiesta or important public event. They are a huge favorite with kids, even though most small children are hesitant to get too close to them.

HOLY WEEK

Holy Week, S*emana Santa*, runs from Palm Sunday to Easter Sunday. It marks the last week of Lent. These dates vary from year to year according to the Ecclesiastical Calendar. Easter is the high point of the liturgical year for the Catholic Church, commemorating the last week of Jesus's life. Article 75 of the Constitution states that Costa Rica is a Catholic country.

In fact, it is a week where very little happens outside of the celebrations. The Government shuts down for the entire week. Most businesses close either for the whole week or at least by noon on Wednesday. Hordes of people head out of the city for a vacation. The beach resorts are all packed. Vacation spots at higher elevations are also very busy. Hotel reservations for this week are hard to come by. Traffic can be a nightmare, even with some lane reversals on major routes to facilitate the exodus and the return home.

In some towns there are spectacular re-enactments of the events leading up to the Crucifixion and, on Easter Sunday, the Resurrection. There are religious organizations in places like Orosi and San Juan de Flores that put on flamboyant public performances that Cecil B. DeMille would find utterly to his liking. Later in the week, the streets are clogged with Biblical characters in costume. There are Roman soldiers in full armor and bright capes; huge crosses lumbering along, replete with ladders, hammers, and nails; and Virgins in period attire atop tables on street corners, holding forth to the spectators. One of the high points comes on Good Friday when the crucified wounded body is carried around town on a litter, sometimes open, sometimes enclosed in glass. You may not be able to drive around town during these times. The streets will be full of Romans, Virgins, Apostles, etc.

On Holy Thursday and Good Friday, Costa Rica has not allowed alcohol sales for many years. Recently, they changed the law to allow local communities to decide whether or not to enforce this prohibition. The national *ley seca*, dry law, forbade all sales of alcohol. This included retail outlets, hotels and restaurants, and tourist resorts across the country. Penalties for violators are stiff. There are illicit sales, but you may be out of luck unless you are known to the seller. If you imbibe, you should ask about this before midnight on Wednesday.

A few years ago during Holy week I was talking about this to some people in a small watering hole in Guanacaste. The owner assured me she would let me in the back door if I wanted a cold one on Thursday or Friday. It turned out a man at the bar was a brewery representative. He told us they sold more beer during Semana Santa than the entire month of December. This is a big vacation week, and there is a great deal of partying. Recently, a high government official got himself in hot water by denigrating the law. He stated that, like every other self-respecting Tico, he knew enough to buy extra supplies in advance. Dry law notwithstanding, it is not a very dry week.

There is one celebratory phase of this week to be avoided. The evening of Holy Saturday is call the *quema de Judas,* the burning of Judas. This is an unsanctioned street happening that entails a lot of beer consumption, fires set in the roadways, vandalism, petty crime, etc. It's really garden variety hooliganism. The police are out in full force that night, but it is widespread. This is a good night to stay in.

THE DAY OF AFRO-COSTA RICAN CULTURE

The City of Limón is known for having three distinct cultures: Afro-Descendents (their preferred term), Chinese, and Whites (again, their preference). The Afro-Descendents speak Spanish, English, and a patois based on English, sometimes called Caribbean Creole. The Chinese speak Chinese and Spanish.

The White-Hispanics generally only speak Spanish unless they are involved in the tourist industry. English is the lingua franca of tourist travel the world over. Some people would argue that immigrant Nicaraguans now constitute a fourth group.

The Spanish brought along some African slaves during the Conquest. However, the majority of Afro-Descendents in Limón trace their families back to Jamaican workers who came to Costa Rica for employment with the railroad. This was a rail line from San José to the port of Limón built by the American Minor C. Keith. It was completed in 1890. There were not enough local workers to meet the company's needs, and the Jamaicans had several advantages. They were accustomed to the hot humid climate; they spoke English; and they were literate and numerate, having gone through the British colonial school system. Some Afro-Descendents proudly display their ancestors' British passports and maintain family connections in Jamaica.

Keith soon realized he did not have enough freight business to make money with the railroad and began the banana business that ultimately became United Fruit. His need for workers grew with the success of the banana trade. He paid the Jamaicans a little more than he paid the local Costa Ricans. His rationale was their education, but many people believe it was an early strategy to prevent the two groups from forming alliances.

August is known as the *Festival de la Cultura Negra*, the Festival of Black Culture. There are many cultural performances and events during the month: speeches, art shows, theater, etc. On the 31st there is a truly beautiful parade, the *Gran Parade de Gala*. Stunning floats depict aspects of Afro-Caribbean culture. It is an enjoyable event for the whole family.

Apart from the parade, it's worth the trip just to see the colorful dresses worn by the women. They are more than happy to allow you to take photographs of them in their finery. The men dress up as well, but they are far more formal.

THE ANNEXATION

Mexico and Central America gained their independence from Spain on September 15, 1821. The news did not reach Costa Rica until October 11th, but Independence Day is still celebrated here on September 15th. Actually, there is a small movement to change the date, but the 15th is still the official holiday.

It took some time for the Central American countries to sort out their governments, borders, and so forth. During the colonial era, the Partido de Nicoya was a separate entity. It had been the first part of Costa Rica conquered and controlled by the Spanish and remained independent from the neighboring colonies of Costa Rica and Nicaragua. There is a common misconception among many people that it was formerly a part of Nicaragua. This was never the case. Ironically, colonial Costa Rica had more involvement with Nicaragua. Nicoya reported directly to the Captaincy General of Guatemala, the Spanish regional administrative center. Costa Rica had to send its reports via León, Nicaragua.

On July 25th, 1824, the Partido elected to join with Costa Rica. This is known as The Annexation, *La Anexión*. It is celebrated every year as a national holiday. In San José there are celebrations of the traditional foods, dance, and folklore of Guanacaste. In Guanacaste there are many civic activities. The President and other politicians visit to make speeches. Streets are decorated with the slogan, "de la Patria por nuestra voluntad." This means Costa Rican by our choice and is on the coat of arms of Nicoya.

There are even big Christmas-like lights with this slogan arching over the main streets.

At the time of independence, the Partido consisted of all of modern-day Guanacaste, minus the townships of Bagaces and Cañas, which were part of Costa Rica. It also included the townships of Lepanto, Paquera, Cóbano, and some islands in the Gulf of Nicoya, which were assigned to the Province of Putarenas by presidential decree in 1915. This was purportedly done due to the difficulty of travel between the upper and lower regions of the Nicoya Peninsula. It was easier to access these places by sea from Puntarenas. However, it remains a sore point in Guanacaste, and there are both court and legislative efforts underway to either rescind this decree or at least hold a referendum. During the Annexation celebrations in Guanacaste, you will see protest signs addressing this controversy.

INDEPENDENCE DAY

Independence Day in Costa Rica begins with a parade on the evening of September 14th with school bands and *faroles*, colorful lanterns or luminaries carried on short staffs by children. Generally, families and teachers march together along a designated route, often ending up at the town park.

The symbolism of the farol is to commemorate Dolores Bedoya who carried a lantern through the streets of Guatemala on the evening of September 14th, 1821, to urge people to support independence.

Preparation starts well in advance. School bands start intense practice by the middle of August and farol makers are hard at work months before. Many children make their own faroles as craft projects.

SANTA CRUZ FIESTAS PATRONALES

Santa Cruz, Guanacaste proudly calls itself The City of Folklore. The *Fiestas Patronales de Santa Cruz* it holds every January are indeed impressive and well worth attending. Hotels in Snata Cruz are booked a year in advance, but there are a number of other towns within reasonable driving distance. The party begins on the evening of the 13th, no matter what the day of the week. This is the eve of the fiesta, but there is plenty going on. There is music, often a free concert in the park, a mascarada with swirling payasos, food, street musicians, etc. The bars do a brisk business.

There is a lot of temporary construction for this event. There is a large stage-altar built by the Parque Bernabela Ramos with an impressive sound system, fresh flowers, seating, etc. In Parque los Mangos, a few blocks to the north, there is a rough wooden bull ring erected each year. That is where you will also find a small village of beer tents and food vendors.

Fiestas Patronales means the fiestas of the patron saint, known in English as The Black Christ of Esquipulas. He is often referred to El Negrito, El Negro, etc. for his dark color. Esquipulas is a town in Guatemala with a similar icon. There it is housed in a full-fledged basilica and is a major destination for religious pilgrimages. His official day is January 15th.

La Entrada del Santo, the arrival of the saint, takes place on the 14th. He leaves the town of Arado, a few miles away, early in the morning. He is carried on a litter with an accompanying procession on his journey into town. One special group in the procession is called the *Indios Promesanos*, the Indian Pilgrims. They are a well organized religious organization of men and women dedicated to honoring the Santo with dancing and song. They dress in traditional rural attire, white clothes with red bandanas, and perform folk dances along the route. Later, they escort him around Santa Cruz as well.

In fact, the poor saint has been shuffled aside a bit for the more popular tope and a display of the bulls being transported in a truck. These events now take place in the Parque Bernabela Ramos while the saint's procession deposits him at a makeshift altar set up in the street a few blocks away. Here, people line up to touch him and pray for his intervention. The larger crowd is following the tope and the bulls to the Parque de los Mangos. Later, he will get to march around town and end up at the large temporary altar in the park for a mass in his honor. In this procession, he is once again the main attraction.

This is an excellent place to see Tico bulls. The ring is rustic, but comfortable. It is small enough so you are close to the action. The only downside is that the best bulls are busy elsewhere at this time. The big bucks draw them to a much more commercial fiesta in Palmares. The Santa Cruz bulls tend to be a little barn sour, but they can still send a little business to the Red Cross EMTs. Be sure to pay attention to the highly skilled horsemen who rope the bulls.

To spare you the confusion, there is more than one saint, at least two. While one is out and about, there is another waiting to hear your prayers for a miracle in front of the church. This icon is famous for its curative powers. You can ask for a cure by purchasing an ex-voto. These are small metal representations of different body parts, and leaving one for the Cristo lets him know which part of your body is in need of his assistance. These are aptly called *milagros* or *promesas*, miracles or promises. Unlike Esquipulas, this church does not display a mountain of testimonial crutches purportedly left by newly ambulatory supplicants.

LIBERIA FIESTAS

Most people only see Liberia because of the international airport. They spend a night there on their way to or from some other part of the country. I find Liberia a very pleasant place to visit in its own right. While it is the largest and most commercial city in Guanacaste, that was not always the case. During colonial times it was considerably smaller and less prosperous than either Nicoya or Santa Cruz. At that time it was called Guanacaste, after the Guanacaste tree. You can see both the tree and the endangered White-tailed Deer on the 1000 colón bill, the smallest denomination of paper currency.

The annual *Fiestas Cívicas de Liberia* is an international event. People come from all over the world to take in this celebration of the cattle culture way of life of Guanacaste. There are concerts, bulls, displays of horsemanship, and displays of Guanacastecan folklore. There are topes and *cimarronas*, small traditional musical groups. There is also a great deal of beer, as in all fiestas. *Chinamos*, food stalls, with fiesta food abound. The ceviche is especially good.

There is also a *diana*, an early morning (5 AM) march or parade. Most people don't get up at the crack of dawn for this: They are still up from the night before.

The bulls at the Liberia event are very good. The Guanacastecans are properly proud of their livestock.

This event takes place the last week of February and the first week of March. Hotels book well ahead of time, so call early for a reservation. Some travel companies offer package tours.

EL REZO DEL NIÑO

Article 75 of the Constitution states that Costa Rica is a Catholic country. That sounds more theocratic than the reality. The majority of Ticos will affirm they are Catholics, but many are rather laid back in their approach to observance and dogma. This is especially true in the areas of relationships, marriage, divorce, birth control, etc. There is an active debate in the country over the role the Church should play today. Negotiations between the Vatican and the Government are underway to update the particulars of the relationship.

One Catholic ritual still very popular is *El Rezo del Niño*, the prayer of the (Christ) child. This is an event that takes place in homes and includes the extended family, friends, neighbors, etc. The clergy plays no role in this observance. It takes place while the *pasitos*, small manger scenes, are still displayed in homes from Christmas. The season for the Rezo starts on January 7th, after Three Kings Day. It runs up to and including the Feast of Candlemas on February 2nd. After this date the pasitos are put away for the year.

Portales are the larger outdoor manger scenes. They can be elaborate scenes with life-sized displays of people and animals. They are well lit and attract a lot of sightseers. People will go on tours of neighborhoods at night to see especially good portales, much like going out in the U.S. to see illuminated Christmas decorations.

The Rezo is a happy festive occasion, a nice family get-together. It takes place in front of the manger scene and is conducted by a *rezador(a)*, moderator (literally, pray-er), male or female. The moderator says the rosary with some explanation of the five mysteries. The audience joins in for some of the prayers. The rezadores are paid for their services.

A simple Rezo might be conducted without music by one rezador. Fancier Rezos may involve a moderator with a good singing voice and several accompanying musicians. In this case there may be some carols or other religious music.

The Rezo is very much a family or neighborhood event. It is not a large gathering and takes place in a home. It is a nice small party with a religious theme, but not so much so as to exclude people uncomfortable with Catholicism.

As with all such events in Costa Rica, there is food. The host family provides food and drink for all in attendance. It is even said some less-than-devout Catholics develop a sudden interest in prayer during this period. They may attend several Rezos each week, perhaps more for the edibles than spiritual reinforcement. Pray often, eat well.

At the end of the event you will likely be given a bag with a few extra goodies to take home. It will be small pastries, little home-made rolls, and such.

February 2nd marks the end of the Rezo season. It always ends before Lent: Ash Wednesday cannot fall earlier than the February 4th. On the 2nd the Pope gives a blessing for the Presentation of the Lord, the infant Jesus, at the temple. Some people watch this on TV, and that is their Rezo. It is also broadcast over the radio. While this may save the cost of the rezador, the host is still on the hook for food and drink.

Bar Food

Costa Rican cuisine has the unfortunate reputation for being bland, boring, and uninspired. People think that Tico food is just rice and beans, fried chicken, and starchy plantains. This is unjustified and unfortunate. There are many traditional dishes that are authentic and enjoyable. *Comida típica* (traditional cooking) which includes such dishes as *olla de carne, tortilla aliñada* and *pescado entero* (pot of meat, cheese tortilla and whole fish) is not only delicious, but also intriguing. These typical foods are more laborious to prepare and are not as commonly found on menus. They may also be suffering from competition with Gringo fast food.

A good way to explore the more interesting and varied side of Costa Rican cooking is to start with bar food. Tantalizing and unusual small dishes (*bocas*) are there for the tasting in countless small establishments around the country. You don't even have to commit to a large meal to try them out. Remember that part of the fun is that they are a little different every place you go: be adventuresome! You should consider your research into this topic a service to culture and humanity.

The offerings are endless and varied. Many bar-restaurants offer very complete menus, including full and half portions of regular meals along with standard side dishes. Following are a few of my favorite bocas.

CHIFRIJO

In my humble opinion, *chifrijo* is the king of Tico bar food. A good chifrijo will attract a steady crowd of eager patrons. Even confirmed teetotalers will sneak into a disreputable gin mill to enjoy the culinary delights of this dish.

It is the only boca that I am aware of that has had a patent taken out by its inventor, Miguel Ángel Cordero Araya. He developed this heavenly recipe in the 1990s at his bar and restaurant (Cordero's) in Tibás, just north of San José. Chifrijo is uniquely Costa Rican fare.

The name was suggested by one of the first customers to try it and is a composite of CHI + FRIJO: the first three letters of three ingredients (*chicharrón, chile* and *chimichurri*) and frijo, from *frijol.*

It is a layered dish, so proportion and structure are important. Harmony among the component layers is critical. Chifrijo is constructed in a bowl as follows:

1) A foundation of white rice is laid down on the bottom of the bowl.
2) Next comes a thick layer of cooked savory beans. Mostly, *frijoles tiernos,* red beans, are used, but *frijoles cubaces* (large beans) are sometimes used as well. The beans are cooked in spices and, to me, are the heart of the dish.
3) The beans are crowned with a portion of chicharrón. Commonly, this is the Costa Rican version of chicharrón, small cooked pieces of meat (*chicharrón de posta*). *Chicharrón crocante* (or *chicharrón de pellejo*) is the crispy pork skin or rind which may also be used.
4) The meat is then smothered in chimichurri or *pico de gallo,* a chopped blend of tomato, cilantro, onion, sweet pepper and lime juice.

5) Tortilla chips are served on the side or tucked into the sides of the bowl.

Additionally, there may be a topping of jalapeño pepper or pieces of avocado. Along with this plate, you will invariably be offered a *chilera*. This is a homemade concoction of chopped hot peppers, carrots, cauliflower, onions, green beans, and sweet peppers that have been pickled in vinegar for several weeks. Don't let an unattractive well-used container put you off this treat. Use the spoon in the jar to scoop out some chunks of spicy vegetables. Tabasco sauce is also commonly used. Chifrijo itself is not *picante* (spicy hot), but you are free to turn up the temperature.

As with all bar food, variety in ingredients, size and presentation is the norm. Commonly, a bar will offer two sizes of chifrijo, a smaller bowl as a boca and a larger version that makes a decent light dinner.

CEVICHE

Chifrijo may be king, but ceviche (now a word in English and many other languages) is the standard by which Tico bar food is judged. It is a dish popular over a wide area of the world, especially Central and South America. Perú considers it part of its National Heritage and has a holiday in its honor. Costa Ricans are very passionate about their ceviche and it is sold in almost all bars, on the street, at roadside stands, and in bulk at seafood restaurants or fish markets. You can even buy ceviche in sealed plastic bags in liquor stores and supermarkets. If you find yourself in an establishment that does not offer it, you may want to reconsider your choice of watering holes.

The serving dishes and portions vary widely. Some places offer just a small glass while most serve it in a small bowl. Some even have the option of a medium sized dish that, with chips or crackers, will prove a heartier snack.

Essentially, ceviche is chopped up raw fish and spices that are "cooked" or pickled in the citric acid of lemon and/or lime juice. A rough standard recipe:

1) Cut fresh white fish into small cubes. Many species are used including sea bass, tilapia, marlin, shark, etc. Mince some onion (red is elegant), sweet pepper, cilantro and garlic.
2) Combine the ingredients and cover them with lemon and or lime juice.
3) Cover and keep refrigerated for at least two hours.

You will also find ceviche made of just shrimp or octopus (more common in retail outlets selling in bulk). Ceviche mixing fish with shrimp or other seafood is called *mixto*. There is also a popular ceviche made of *pianguas*, clams. Ceviche de pianguas is dark and quite different than other ceviches.

Ceviche is served with tortilla chips or soda crackers. For picante lovers who ordinarily do not like the vinegar base of Tabasco, this is an exception as the vinegar blends wonderfully with the citric base.

VUELVE A LA VIDA

This is a very upscale ceviche. It will run you double the price of regular fish ceviche, or close to it. It contains at least fish, clams, shrimp and either squid or octopus.

Vuleve a la vida means "come back (or return) to life." Many people say this is a reference to the reputed efficacy of this dish as a cure for hangovers or illness. A professional ceviche seller assures me it really alludes to power of the dish to increase sexual potency, a natural Viagra. It is not a biblical allusion to Lazarus or Easter.

This dish is found in many forms in many countries and it's often seen as a *tour de force* of the chef. Here it is occasionally served as a hot seafood soup with roughly the same ingredients.

If you are a seafood lover, you should jump at the chance to try either variety. Give your ceviche habit a night off and go for a little resurrection.

TACOS AND GALLOS

As a student in Mexico, I ate street tacos several times a week. They were fresh hot soft corn tortillas filled with healthy portions of pork bits, cilantro, chopped onion and hot sauce. After realizing that I had wolfed down five dog tacos, I learned to always look for the reassuring fresh pig's head in the window. Hard tacos were only served in fancier restaurants, often with elegant toppings of sour cream and guacamole. Today, tacos have become international fare. Variety in form and ingredients is the rule rather than the exception.

Tico tacos are hard tacos and almost always use a wheat flour tortilla. They can hold anything in the way of meat, chicken, fish, cheese, beans, etc. Most are made with the tortilla completely rolled around the contents, while others are partially open like taco shells. They are generally fried along with the filling and may have an additional topping of ground beans, cheese, sour cream or salad. Some bars offer fried mini tacos using corn tortilla wrappers. If you are not a big ketchup and mayo fan, you should stipulate that you would like them on the side.

A boca that generates considerable confusion among visitors is the *gallo*. This is simply a soft warm corn tortilla with pieces of chicken, meat, or some other filling. Many foreigners make the mistake of thinking that the Costa Rican gallo is a taco. Any Tico will quickly set you straight that the tortilla used in a taco wraps all the way around and overlaps itself, while the tortilla in a gallo folds like a slice of bread; the edges come together evenly and must be held upright between the thumb and the forefinger. It resembles a tortilla hammock or sling. If you have a fondness for losing arguments, try telling a local that it's really a taco. In truth, only one thing matters regarding gallos: they're delicious.

HUEVO DE TORTUGA

The consumption of *huevo de tortuga* or turtle egg is extremely controversial. There is a legal harvest of Olive Ridley turtle eggs on the Pacific coast. Only the early nests are raided on the premise that these eggs do not survive the heat of dry season and subsequent waves of nesting females. Another argument for this practice is that it reduces the price of turtle eggs and discourages poaching. It provides income for local residents and has contributed to town improvements such as schools.

In fact, demand far exceeds the legal supply and there is a thriving black market for illegally collected eggs. Recently, there was an armed robbery of eggs from a turtle conservation station on the Caribbean side, where all harvesting is illegal. There are regular reports of poachers being caught transporting large quantities of illicit eggs.

Turtle eggs are traditionally seen as enhancing male virility, so they are consumed almost exclusively by men. The main market also seems to be the Central Valley. This is very much a bar practice.

Normally, they are served raw with *sangrita,* a tomato-based drink that may also include orange juice, hot pepper, other fruit or ginger ale. The egg is then swallowed without chewing, in one gulp.

My opinion: buying turtle eggs promotes poaching and threatens turtle survival. You will have to make this decision for yourself. Until there is a truly regulated market, I will not partake of the leathery little globes.

NACHOS

Sadly, *nachos* in Costa Rica are the ugly duckling that never blossoms into a swan: a case of arrested development. They lack the melted cheese, jalapeño slices, chili beans and such that make this dish so decadently delicious. They are commonly offered plain or with chicken or meat pieces sprinkled on top of the chips. They are usually served at room temperature and may be topped with a shredded cheese like Mozzarella. There may be chopped tomatoes or lettuce as well. Often they bear additional toppings of *natilla* (liquid sour cream), mayo or perhaps ketchup. As with all bocas, recipe diversity is the rule. Unfortunately, in this case appetizing is the exception.

I had always thought they were a U.S. Tex-Mex (a legitimate cuisine in its own right) creation. In fact, nachos are Mexican, but just barely. They were invented in Piedras Negras, Mexico, across the border from Eagle Pass, Texas. On an afternoon in

1943 a group of US Army wives returning from a shopping trip stopped in a restaurant there. The maître d', Ignacio "Nacho" Anaya, scrambled to make them a snack with what he had on hand after a busy day. He called it "*Nacho's Especiales*" and the name evolved from there.

The dish soon became popular on the US side of the border and spread out from Texas to the entire country. Ironically, they probably made their way back south to Mexican resorts due to U.S. tourists asking for them. Today, they are all but universal.

You can find good nachos in some resort towns and maybe in some upscale establishments in the Central Valley, especially the western suburbs known collectively as Gringo Gulch. However, this is one boca that you might want to pass on in traditional Tico bars.

PATÍ

Patí is a small pastry, a turnover, filled with a mixture of ground beef, onion, spices and a touch of hot pepper, often the hot Panama Chile, all cooked in oil. It is not really very hot, at least not to my picante-loving mouth. You will find them in rectangular and half-round shapes. They are very oily and you will quickly see evidence of this if you buy them in paper.

Patí is another snack like enyucados and burritos that you may have to find near a bar, rather in than inside. They are very common street food on the Caribbean side and you can find them there well into the evening in small stands with glass cases. Any festival in Limón Province will have multiple patí venders. Central Valley bakeries also sell them, usually in small paper bags of two.

VIGORÓN

This is a very different plate that can make a fairly good meal. In some countries it is used as a late dinner or a very early breakfast.

Vigorón is a dish constructed around a mound of cabbage salad. The cabbage is dressed with a sauce of tomatoes, onions, cilantro, and lime juice. Salt, pepper, sugar and cumin may be added to the dressing as well. Arranged around it, usually in a nice star pattern, are long pieces of cooked *yuca* (cassava) and chicharrón crocante, crispy pork rind. There may also be guacamole.

CHALUPAS

This is a messy delight that you should attack with fingers, fork, knife, and several reserve napkins. The foundation of a *chalupa* is a crispy fried corn tortilla. The superstructure is infinitely varied, but often consists of a hearty first layer of ground beans, refried beans in Gringo speak. The beans are followed by a tier of meat, chicken, cheese or chicharrón. This is crowned by a big pile of lettuce or shredded cabbage. Unless you request otherwise, it will likely be slathered with ketchup and mayo.

Interestingly, the term "refried beans" is a mistaken translation, one that will never be remedied. In fact, the beans are only fried once in the process. The prefix *re-* in Spanish means a repetition, just as in English. However, *re-* is also a modifier that means very or well. The proper translation from Mexican Spanish for *frijoles refritos* is really well-fried beans. This problem is moot in Costa Rica as here they are called *frijoles molidos* or ground beans. Ground beans here may be red or black.

MORCILLA

Morcilla is blood sausage, blood pudding (British), *moronga* (Mexican) or *blutwurst* (German, older German-American). It is not as popular in Costa Rica as in Spain or Mexico, but you will find it on many bar boca menus. Any source of blood can be used, but pig is by far the most common.

Tico morcilla is milder in taste and less aromatic than other varieties, but still very good. It is usually served chopped up and fried with onions, sweet peppers and other flavorings. You can have it served on rice or in gallos. It is a rich dark mixture that makes for a comforting and filling meal.

Many people cringe at the thought of eating blood, but travel eating is supposed to be an adventure. Try splitting a plate with a companion or ask for a very small serving. It cannot possibly be worse than the unmentionables that go into hot dogs.

YUCA

Yuca, or cassava, is a common component of bar bocas, as in vigorón. However, it warrants some special attention as probably the best belly ballast for imbibing you can find. A little yuca in your system will help you soldier through the toughest pub crawl. *Yuca frita* is simply small chunks of yucca deep fried. It does not take up the oil like french fries and sits very comfortably in your stomach. It is also far tastier and a small plate can easily be shared by two or more people.

Enyucados are not always sold inside bars, but can often be found nearby in small sodas or stands with glass cases on the street, even well into the evening. This is a fried ball of cassava dough that may have a meaty center. It's not very greasy and is quite substantial. This delicacy gets my vote for the best street snack or finger food in Costa Rica.

SQUID RINGS

I am a serious lover of all things squid. If there were pistachio-squid ice cream, I would give it a try. Squid rings are my favorite.

Aros de calamar, squid rings, are not found in every bar in the country. You will have better luck closer to the ocean, on either coast. Upscale establishments in the central valley may have them as well. As always, you have to be very careful to ask if they are the frozen commercial nightmares that should be avoided at all costs. I call this freezer-fryolator food.

Local fresh squid from the kitchen of a good cook is a treasure worth seeking out.

PICADILLO

Picar in Spanish means to chop or mince. *Picadillo* is a snack or side dish made of chopped vegetables, mostly starches. It may also contain meat, especially beef, but that is not essential. The main ingredient is usually small cubes of potato. Chayote, carrots, squash, *arracache* (arracacha, white carrot), tomatoes, and other vegetables may be used as well. It is spiced with garlic, onions, sweet red peppers, cilantro, and oregano.

Picadillo is served in a small bowl with rice or on a plate in tortillas to make gallos. It has a comforting mild taste and a soft texture. Ticos see it as very festive.

BURRITOS

A Tico *burrito* is a fried envelope or packet of wheat tortilla with a stuffing of beans, meat, cheese, chicken, chicharrón, etc. It can be a bit greasy, but makes a good medium level snack. Often you will have to satisfy a burrito craving from a stand near the bar of the same sort that sells enyucados.

BAGGED BOCAS

Most bars will offer an assortment of bagged crunchy nibbles in addition to their kitchen bocas. You will find peanuts and cashews. Plantain chips are very common and come in *verde* or green, a lighter more yellow chip, and *maduro* or ripe, a darker somewhat sweeter version. These chips are made from a starch plantain, not the sweet banana Americans are used to. They often have salt and lime added for flavor. Potato chips are common and you may find cassava chips as well. The cassava or yuca chips are lighter and seem to absorb less oil than potato chips. Pork rinds are sold in bags, although not as commonly as in Mexico or the U.S.

CONDIMENTS

Mayonnaise and ketchup are universally offered and used, liberally, on almost everything. Two things to remember: the yellow squeeze bottle is mayo, not mustard; Costa Rican ketchup is much sweeter than the U.S. version. Homemade chilera is common, as is Tabasco sauce. *Chilero* (hot sauce) is often available as well. Salsa Lizano is a ubiquitous table sauce that is made from "natural spices and vegetables" according to a secret family recipe. Lizano is a little sweet and sometimes compared to Worcestershire. You will generally have to request salt or pepper.

Costa Rica may never have the reputation for its small dishes that Spain does for *tapas*, but it's time for Tico bocas to step out of the shadows and let the world know how good they really are.

Bar Soup

Bar soup is a category of bar food. I treat it separately simply because it strikes North Americans so exceedingly odd to go for an ice-cold beer and a piping hot bowl of soup. Nonetheless, it is very Costa Rican.

In Costa Rica, *sopa*, soup, does not come out of a can to be mixed with milk or water. Had he lived here, Andy Warhol would have had to paint bottles of Salsa Lizano. Soup is all home made, or restaurant-bar made, as the case may be. Like other bar food, soups vary widely from one watering hole to the next. They are served very hot, ambient temperature notwithstanding.

Soups in Costa Rica with a milk base are called *cremas*. You may see a category on menus titled, "Sopas y Cremas." They are all soups, there is just a distinction made for those with milk. Of the soups listed below, only the seafood soup is commonly offered as a crema.

So, get in touch with your inner Tico and order up a beer *bajo cero* (below zero, 0° C. = 32° F.) along with a steaming bowl of soup. Think of the temperature juxtaposition as being like that of a hot fudge sundae.

SOPA AZTECA

The ancient Aztecs were a terribly bloody lot. They were devout in their belief that the sun might neglect to rise if they failed to rip still-beating hearts out of hapless captives on a daily basis.

That may well be the inspiration for the name of this richly red tomato dish, Aztec Soup.

Like the tomato soup my mother made for me as a child, this is true comfort food. Along with the rich tomato base, there are usually plenty of tortilla strips and maybe some pasta. Often there is some chicken and pieces of avocado. Some places will top the soup with shredded cheese. It typically comes in a large bowl and is served very hot.

SOPA NEGRA

Sopa negra, or black soup, is a black bean soup. It is generally a thinner soup than similar recipes in other countries, such as Cuban black bean soup. It is spiced with onions, *culantro coyote* (an herb with the taste of cilantro, but a flat mini-romaine lettuce looking leaf), and, often, oregano. It is not spicy hot or overpowering in flavor.

Sopa negra is served with an egg: hard boiled and sliced into the serving bowl or cracked open raw and cooked directly in the pot of simmering soup. I find hard boiled eggs more visually appealing.

Frequently, this soup will be served with a side of rice. You can spoon in as much or as little as you like.

For men suffering prostate problems, I would ask in advance about the oregano content. Massive amounts of oregano can be the lazy cook's answer to a lack of flavor in all manner of bean dishes.

SOPA DE MARISCOS

Seafood soup, or chowder, is made all over the world. The contents vary everywhere according to what is available in the way of the recent catch. In Costa Rica, the most common ingredients are fish pieces, (often more than one type), clams, and shrimp. If you find a lot of shrimp in your bowl, you are eating above my pay grade. There may also be squid, octopus, or other treats as well.

If you are told that your bowl has *camarón del río* (river shrimp), it means mudbugs, crayfish, crawdads. Salt water shrimp are far more common, but some people are passionate in their preference for crayfish.

This can be a wonderful dish or a terrible disappointment. I would recommend ordering it in a place that has an obvious investment in seafood. Otherwise, it may be watery and very short on real seafood, maybe a few sad frozen clams lurking at the bottom of the bowl.

SUSTANCIA

Sustancia is a consomme often served as a complimentary bar snack. The broth can be made from beef, chicken, or fish. It is served in a small bowl and very hot. It may arrive in front of you unannounced, with no explanation or questions. Generally, everybody at the bar will be served a cup at the same time.

You can also order a larger bowl of sustancia. It is usually served with enough rice to make it a substantial boca.

VUELVE A LA VIDA

Generally, this refers to a very upscale ceviche, or seafood cocktail, with fish, clams, shrimp and either octopus or squid. In Costa Rica, it is also sometimes a hot seafood soup. The difference between sopa de mariscos and vuelve a la vida is perhaps academic. The latter is less common, often still appearing on menus in establishments that in reality no longer serve the dish. I suspect this is due to the cost of maintaining the stock of expensive ingredients. Vuelve generally has a greater variety of seafood; it is more likely to have squid or octopus and will cost more than a bowl of sopa de mariscos. That said, the contents of both vary widely dependent on the cost and availability of different seafood, not to mention the personal taste of the cook.

Vuleve a la vida means "come back (or return) to life". Many people say this is a reference to the reputed efficacy of this dish as a cure for hangovers or illness. A professional ceviche seller assures me it really alludes to power of the dish to increase sexual potency, a natural Viagra. It is not a biblical allusion to Lazarus or Easter.

If you love seafood, you should jump at the opportunity for either variety of resurrection. They both provide for a substantial meal.

Fiesta Food

Costa Rica is awash with fiestas, large and small, at all times of the year. Every small town has its *fiestas patronales* or *fiestas cívicas*. Also, many have religious festivals such as Holy Week, The Black Christ of Esquipulas, etc. There are national events as well such as the *Tope Nacional* (National Horse Parade in San José on December 26th); the *Toros* in Zapote, starting on December 25th, running until the first week of January and telecast nationally; the *Virgen de los Ángeles* on August 2nd.

Originally, many of the town fiestas were *turnos*, community fairs organized for the purpose of raising money for charitable or community projects. The term turnos comes from the towns taking turns in the scheduling of the events. The term is still used, at least for smaller events.

These fiestas are very much family oriented and one thing every member of the family expects is fiesta food, and lots of it. I have yet to see U.S. fair delicacies such as deep-fried Twinkies, but Tico fiesta food can be wonderfully decadent in its own right.

The stands that sell these delicacies are called *chinamos*. For large events, the contract negotiations for the concessions may be very competitive, with progress reported in the newspaper.

CHORREADAS

Chorreadas are basically tender uncooked corn, cut off the cob. The kernels are roughly ground up, perhaps with some egg, into a coarse batter. Corn starch is added as a thickener. Chorreadas fall into two categories: *dulce* and *salada,* sweet and salty. The offerings at fiestas are almost always sweet, not extremely so. In fact, salada does not really mean salty in taste, just not sweet. In either case, they are then grilled, like pancakes and served with *natilla* (a liquid form of sour cream).

An important distinction is the color of the corn. Fresh yellow corn is seen as giving the best color and flavor. However, white corn is less expensive and can be dyed, even purchased already colored. My Tico friends assure me they can quickly tell the difference, but I am still trying to refine my taste buds in this area.

ELOTE

Elote is just corn on the cob, but not the sweet corn Americans are so fond of. It is regular starch corn, what my grandparents used to call cow corn. It is a little tough, but very enjoyable. You will see it often in shallow pans of yellow margarine, sometimes being rotated by a mechanical arm.

PUPUSA

Pupusa is really a Salvadorean concoction that is becoming increasingly popular in Costa Rica. I am starting to see more *pupuserías* (pupusa outlets) opening up. Everybody knows what they are from the fiestas. You can even buy frozen pupusas in the supermarket and they aren't all that bad.

It is a thick coarse tortilla made with a stuffing of refried beans and/or cheese. In the pupusa shops you can order fancier fillings and toppings like fried meat or tomato sauce.

CHICHARRÓN

There are two versions of *chicharrón* in Costa Rican cuisine and both are found at fiestas. First, *chicharrón de pellejo* is what people familiar with Mexican food know as chicharrón. It is heavy pork rind, the skin of the pig deep fried until it is very crispy and crunchy. In fact, it is also known here as *chicharrón crocante*, crunchy chicharrón. Watch your teeth with this as it can be very hard to bite off a piece.

Chicharrón de posta is more commonly what Ticos mean when they talk about chicharrón. It consists of fatty pieces of pork that have been deep fried until they are rather tough and chewy. The size of the pieces ranges from about ½ inch square up to a chunk between the size of a golf ball and a baseball. I doubt your arteries would thank you for a steady diet of chicharrón, either variety, but they are well worth an occasional splurge. The tough texture of both types is just a bonus: It's fun food to eat.

PINCHOS

Pinchos are enticing shish kebabs grilled over charcoal. They are usually beef, pork or chicken, but sometimes you might have the good fortune to find skewered shrimp. Generally, they are marinated for 24 hours in advance. Often there is a choice in the final grilling sauce for your pincho, *picante* (spicy hot) or not. They are served upright, napkin on the bottom, often with a full or half tortilla on the top of the stick. The tortilla serves as much to help you attack this treat neatly as it is part of the dish.

Some pincho stands will make use of the fire to offer pieces of grilled *salchichón*, a common mild sausage. These may be put on a stick or just sold with a tortilla to wrap around the meat.

The stands are themselves worth a look. They range from tiny grills made from an old wheel rim to elaborate structures, mobile and stationary, with shade, coolers, glass fronts, and other amenities.

PARRILLA

At bigger events I see large open grills fired by wood, charcoal or gas. These stands offer a variety of grilled meat. You can order ribs, chops, and salchichón. There may also be *chorizos*, small spicy sausages (Mexican chorizo can be spicy hot). This is more expensive fiesta food.

GREEN MANGOS

Green mangos (or *mangas*, same taste, but a larger fruit) are served in a very creative way, with an impressive menu of condiments and sauces. The mangos are peeled by a small machine resembling an apple peeler. The machine is also used to produce long strips of fruit that pile up nicely in a paper container. You are then faced with the daunting choice of what to add. Lime and salt are always offered, but bigger stands will provide everything from Italian salad dressing to sugary syrups.

Mangos are also commonly sold by walking street vendors. In this case, they are already peeled and sliced into strips. The strips are packaged in small clear plastic bags. The vendor will still offer you at least salt and lime.

CHURROS

At the risk of calling down Tico lightening on my head, let me state that I am not an avid *churro* fan. I simply do not have a sweet tooth. That said, they are a mainstay of fiesta food.

Churros start with a batter of flour, butter, sugar, eggs, vanilla, etc. They are then extruded into star-shaped (cross section) strips four to eight inches long. These strips are deep fried in oil and then powdered with sugar and cinnamon. The fiesta stands offering churros have some very fancy mechanical extruders and large vats of boiling oil.

Small churro stands are common all year long, but are more active during fiestas or holidays. Churros are much better fresh: They do not travel as well as doughnuts. I am told you can make them at home using a frosting extruder.

MORE COMMON FARE

The fiesta food stands also offer a wide variety of more common dishes. You will see huge heaping piles of *arroz con pollo* (rice with chicken, always a safe bet), *arroz cantonés* (Cantonese rice, often just called cantonés, with bits of fried pork) or chop suey. You can always fall back on the ever popular fried chicken.

Please see the chapter on Traditional Tico Cuisine for more information on the above dishes.

TAMALES

The Costa Rican *tamal* (the singular in Spanish is tamal - tamale is English) is a work of art, wondrous to behold, and a culinary epiphany to consume. They are not always found at fiestas and fairs, but are an essential part of the Christmas holidays. Many families will make a large number of them before Christmas and try to keep them from being eaten too quickly. Everybody loves them. The guard at my condo is fond of calling the winds that buffet the San José region around Christmas *vientos tamaleros*, tamale winds. They are more properly known as the *vientos navide-ños*, Christmas winds.

The task of cooking up a big batch of tamales is long and arduous. I took an intensive seminar in the process with some fairly traditional Tico friends a couple years ago. They started around 5 AM, well before my arrival. It was solid work until 5 PM, when the first batch of 50 went into a huge pot of boiling water over a wood fire in an open area behind their house. This first batch came out at 6 PM. They made 5 batches that day.

Unlike the tiny Mexican tamale wrapped in corn husks or the enormous Columbian variety that must go at least a pound, the Tico version is the perfect size for a light meal or a solid snack. The ones you buy in the supermarket (year around) weigh 500 grams for 2, about 8 ½ ounces each. Some chinamos or bars will offer smaller tamales. They are made, cooked, and sold as a pair, called a *piña*, tied together with string. You can buy just one for immediate consumption at restaurants or stands.

The Tico tamal is wrapped in large leaves, sometimes called banana leaf, but actually one of several other plants. Collecting these leaves is a seasonal source of income for some rural people. It is not an endeavor free of risk. Last year a collector was bitten by a poisonous snake. The viper must have hit a vein because the poor guy sat down and died on the spot.

There is a little meat in the tamal, generally pork and/or chicken. This is the first step, to boil up the meat in some spices. The corn is also boiled and then ground into a dough called *masa*. There are small mills that will do the grinding for you. You just have to lug the wet boiled corn to them and bring home the heavy bag of masa. The entire family is put to work assembling the tamales, under the watchful eye of Mom. Proper proportion and structure are critical.

Along with the masa, each tamal gets several other ingredients: a small piece of meat, potato, chick peas, carrots, peas, rice, etc. Everybody has their own preferred recipe. The tamales are then carefully and artfully folded so as not to let the goodies leak out during the cooking. This was not a task I was entrusted with (well, they let me try a couple and then refolded them). Two are then tied together with string to make a piña. The assembled green packets are then boiled for 45 minutes to an hour. A wood fire is traditional.

Traditional Tico Cuisine

Comida típica, or traditional food, includes bar food and fiesta food. Really, all of the food in Costa Rica is typical, except for the recent invasion of international chains hawking extra-cheese pizza (stuffed and piled everywhere), triple-tier burgers with double cheese and extra bacon, US style Tex-Mex with tortilla-ground meat-cheese combinations no Mexican national ever heard of, etc. The ubiquitous small *pollo frito*, fried chicken, outlets have become a part of the national landscape and should now be considered entirely Tico.

In this chapter I will attempt to give a brief, by no means complete, overview of the sorts of dishes you will encounter in more traditional restaurants, including the innumerable small establishments called *sodas*. In some cases the only difference between a *boca*, snack, and a *plato fuerte*, main dish, is the size. Some of these dishes are also commonly served at fiestas, and the difference is simply the setting.

OLLA DE CARNE

If there were a national Costa Rican dish, it would be *olla de carne*, pot of meat. This dish traces its origins back to a Jewish dish called *adafina* and the traditional Spanish *olla podrida*. Olla podrida is often saddled with the unappetizing mistranslation of rotten pot. In fact, the term means powerful pot or strong pot in old Spanish. Don Quixote was not so demented as to fail to appreciate this dish.

This is a wonderful dish that varies widely in its ingredients. It is generally not found on the daily menu of most restaurants due to the time and labor of its preparation. Some places will advertise olla de carne on certain days of the week or just at special times of the year.

Essentially, olla de carne is a soup-stew with beef that is simmered for a long time. Added to the delicious broth are at least several vegetables from a long list. This list includes potatoes, cassava, chayote, squash, green or ripe plantains, carrots, short sections of corn on the cob (not sweet corn), *tiquisque, ñampí, arracache*, (3 starchy roots), etc. It is characteristic of the dish that the vegetables are cut into fairly large and long pieces. It can be very difficult to determine exactly what the chunks are. I recently ordered olla de carne with a group of Tico friends and quickly found everybody's spoon in my bowl trying to guess what the vegetables were. We had to ask the owner to settle the discussion.

Olla de carne is usually served in a large bowl and very hot. It is a meal unto itself with plenty of meat and carbohydrates. This is a must-try for anybody interested in traditional Costa Rican cuisine.

LENGUA EN SALSA ROJA

Lengua en salsa roja, tongue in red sauce, is a common and fairly festive food in Costa Rica. Many of my Tico friends serve it for family gatherings. It is much easier to prepare for a large group than olla de carne.

The tongue is cooked until quite tender and sliced. The ingredients for the sauce vary, but always include plenty of spices such as celery, garlic, onion, cilantro, sweet pepper, paprika, etc. The red color comes from a tomato base and, perhaps paprika or red sweet pepper. There is no hot chile or hot paprika. It is a very mild tasting and pleasant dish with a smooth texture.

Americans often turn up their noses at tongue. That always reminds my of a joke I heard as a child. A client walks into a restaurant and asks after the special. He is told the special of the day is tongue. He responds, "Oh no, I could never eat anything that came out of an animal's mouth. I'll have the three-egg omelet." My 7 year old sense of humor thought that was endlessly funny.

PESCADO ENTERO

This is a dish found in all of Costa Rica, although cookbooks assign its origin to the Caribbean coast. It is very simply a whole fried fish, head and tail intact. Red snapper, grouper, sea bass or croaker are seen as the best, but other fish will do.

Pescado entero is served hot and very crispy. It's fried well enough that it takes a little work to pry the meat off the bones, but that's part of the delight of the meal. It's a little work, but that makes it fun food to eat, like lobster in the shell. Usually, it is served with cassava, rice or fries, and some cabbage or lettuce salad.

Many restaurants will offer you several fish of varying sizes and species, at different prices.

This is another dish shunned by some travelers because they don't like the eyes, but one I consider a great treat. The presentation itself is quite impressive.

Jack Donnelly

GALLO PINTO

Gallo pinto or spotted rooster is the dish most foreigners associate, often in a denigrating tone, with Costa Rican cuisine. Some will go so far as to state that Tico cuisine <u>is</u> gallo pinto, and little else. Gallo pinto is usually shortened to just pinto. These unfortunate souls have simply failed to properly explore the culinary landscape of the country. This is a deficiency I am trying to remedy in these pages.

Pinto is a mixture of rice and beans with some spices such as onion, cilantro, garlic, sweet pepper, Salsa Lizano, etc. It is standard breakfast fare in countless sodas around the country. In fact, it is a dish common, under a variety of names, to all of Latin America and the Caribbean. In different regions, different types of beans are favored. Here, the beans are red or black, mostly black. There are also both red with white and black with white roosters that present the spotted or variegated plumage similar to the appearance of pinto.

Many years ago in Belize, then British Honduras, I was talking to an elderly local lady about this dish. In Belize it is simply called rice and beans, and prepared Caribbean style with coconut milk. Hoping for some more local color, I was pressing her for another name for the dish. She finally told me there was another term. When I eagerly asked her for this name, her face took on a mischievous smile and she answered, "We also call it beans and rice." Okay, I was asking for it.

In Costa Rican sodas, you can order your breakfast pinto with a variety of accompaniments. Commonly, you can have it with fried eggs, soft or well cooked; scrambled eggs, plain or with tomato and/or ham (*huevos fritos tiernos/bien cocidos; huevos revueltos con tomate/jamón*).

I should point out that poached eggs are not standard fare in Costa Rica. A couple years ago an ex of mine came to visit and insisted on ordering a poached egg. After several attempts with different methods (the microwave was an especially bad idea), the soda gave her an egg that was very well cooked, by some technique or another. Fortunately, the owner was a friend of mine, and we had a good laugh over it. We still refer to the her as *el huevo poché*, the poached egg.

Eggs over easy is another challenge. Some places will proudly tell you they can make them. In my experience, the over is easy, but the easy is hard. Obviously, upscale resort hotels may have a handle on both poached and over easy eggs. Huevos frios tiernos will come with the egg white on top fully cooked, and the yolk liquid. During the frying process, the cooks scoop a little hot oil onto the top of the egg to cook the white before the yolk gets hard.

Another hearty choice is to have your pinto with *carne en salsa*, meat in sauce. This is a substantial addition to the pinto and consists of beef that has been simmered in sauce for some time. It's a little like pot roast in a tomato and onion sauce. Be careful ordering this dish, especially in rural areas: you may get far more food than you really want. Some sodas will give you option of a *medio plato*, a half dish, for a little more than half the price of a full plate.

Another common companion to pinto is *salchichón*, a large reddish beef sausage. You may see it sold in big loops. It is not spicy or terribly greasy and has a good flavor. Again, in some sodas you will get more salchichón than you can eat. I once got a serving so large I was praying for a stray dog to pass by.

Chorizo is a smaller and spicier sausage, not always available. It will run you a little more than the salchichón. You won't get a huge portion of chorizo. There may be more than one variety, and the Mexican chorizo may be a little spicy hot.

Chicken is also often served with pinto. It is usually a leg or some other smallish piece stewed in sauce.

One of my favorites is pinto with *queso frito*, fried cheese. This is a semi-hard white cheese, made specifically for frying. It is cooked in oil and served in rectangular slices.

Finally, you can get your pinto with *natilla*, a popular kind of watery sour cream. Many places will give you a small side of natilla with any breakfast, and some will add a piece of white cheese on your plate as well. A piece of fried plantain is also commonly included.

To round out the large traditional breakfast you will be given either tortillas or bread. It is important to ask about this: you may have a choice. In most places the tortillas will be commercial products out of bags (*tortilla de paquete*), but these are actually pretty good. In some rural areas, especially Guanacaste, you may get a heartier handmade tortilla or a half of one (*tortilla palmeada*). Outside of upscale tourist areas, the toasted bread or *tostada* will be *pan cuadrado*, square bread (aptly named). This is commercial white bread from the supermarket. It is rarely well toasted, more like dry-warmed.

CASADO

In tourist or hotel areas, you may see signs advertising breakfast specials outside of restaurants. Be a little careful with these as they may play games with the foreign trade (high-priced coffee not included, etc.). However, sodas are far more likely to advertise the prices of their *casados*, a kind of mixed plate. Casado means married and it is a marriage of several different foods on one large plate.

If you order a casado, you will be asked to choose a meat, chicken or fish portion. The rest of the plate is determined by the soda. It will generally have white rice (not mixed with beans), black (sometimes red) beans, lettuce or cabbage salad, and some additional starch. This can be pasta, macaroni salad, cassava, potatoes, fries, almost anything. You may get bread (usually square) or tortillas as well. This is a very heavy meal. It is not conducive to an active afternoon.

CANTONÉS

Cantonés means Cantonese. When I first arrived in Costa Rica and saw this on the menu of a soda it was in capital letters and did not have the accent on the e. I thought it meant *cantones*, a Costa Rican term for municipalities or counties. Needless to say, I felt the perfect Gringo idiot asking what sort of dish "counties" was. Please feel free to thank me for sparing you this mortification.

Cantonés is a rice dish with well fried bits of pork mixed in. It is usually a plato fuerte, the main course. The rice is fried, darkened, and flavored with soy and spices. It is common fare in sodas, home cooking, and fiesta food. I find it to be filling comfort food.

ARROZ CON POLLO

Rice with chicken is a dish familiar to many Americans. It consists of rice with pieces of shredded chicken. It also contains onion, sweet pepper, pimiento, celery, tomato, carrot, garlic, pepper, cumin, Worcestershire Sauce, and other spices. You may be fortunate enough to find such treasures as peas, olives, and/or raisins.

I particularly like arroz con pollo at fiestas and when traveling. Large bus-stop restaurants usually have this in their hot buffet offerings, and I think it makes for good travel food. It can also be a reasonable-cost option if you should get dragged by friends to an upscale restaurant beyond your means.

CHOP SUEY

Chop suey is chop suey the world over. Trying to pin it down reminds me of the famous quote from the U.S. Supreme Court on pornography: "I shall not attempt further to define . . ., but I know it when I see it." It is surprisingly common and popular in Costa Rica. You will find it almost everywhere.

As in other countries, it is an olio of bean sprouts, noodles, pieces of pork, chicken, prepared meats (bacon, bologna, salami, etc.), soy sauce, onion, assorted vegetables, etc.

My opinion is that this dish is rarely bad and almost never very good. It's pretty much always all right, but never inspiring. I realize some people love it, but I am not one of them.

EMPANADA

For a lighter meal in a soda or to carry out from many small bakeries or stands, the *empanada* is standard fare. It is a stuffed half-moon pastry that is baked or fried in oil. It may contain chicken, beef, cheese, beans, or a variety of sweeter fillings.

If you purchase an empanada in a bakery, it will probably be a baked puff pastry with a filling. Chicken and meat are common options.

If you order an empanada in a soda, it will more likely be made of corn dough and fried in oil. Here, you will usually be limited to fillings of cheese and/or beans. It will be served very hot. You can ask for it *arreglada*, fixed up, and it will be opened to insert some shredded cabbage and mayo, possibly ketchup.

PRENSADA

A *prensada* is a type of fried sandwich made with two tortillas. It usually has a slab of cheese. The fried tortillas and the soft hot cheese make for a pleasant texture. They are not very big, so I order two prensadas for a light meal. I make them at home with cheese, refried beans, tomato, hot sauce, etc.

POLLO FRITO

Fried chicken outlets are everywhere in Costa Rica. Some are small chains, others just mom-and-pop holes in the wall. A lot of it is for take out, but many places have a few tables as well. You can call and have it delivered by motorcycle if you like. It is hot, greasy, sometimes salty, quick, and unavoidable.

Many years ago I worked for a not-to-be-named large corporation in the far south of the country. An expat who owned a small restaurant in town was making a large investment in deep fryers to offer fried chicken. We all thought he was the proverbial fool heading toward the fork in the road with his money. What sort of craziness was it to think Costa Ricans would eat fried chicken? If the grease didn't do him in, I'm guessing he owned that town before long.

If you succumb, and most of us do from time to time, ask for a *porción de pollo*, a portion of chicken. This will get you a bag with a breast and either a leg or a wing. You will also be offered or given a small bag with pieces of plantain or green jalapeños. You may also get a package of two or more tortillas.

COMIDA RÁPIDA

Many sodas will have a section of the menu called *comida rápida*, fast food. It will have burgers, fries, sandwiches, etc. If you order a burger, it will come loaded with a thin slice of ham, lettuce, tomato, mayo (lots of mayo), etc. It is a slippery sandwich and a very messy meal. I like to spice it up with a little hot sauce.

DRINKS

A fixed price casado, and some other meals, will include a drink. This will usually be a *refresco, refresco natural*, commonly called just a *fresco*. It is water and liquefied fruit, often with sugar added. Fruits commonly used in frescos include pineapple, papaya, melon, raspberry, cas (a small bitter fruit), mango, etc. You should be mindful of the level of sweetness: Ticos are very fond of sugar.

The term fresco natural may also be relative. Many places will chop up fresh fruit for the blender and are entirely truthful in calling their drinks natural. Others use *pulpa*, commercially processed fruit. You will want to ask about both the fruit and the sugar.

A *batido* is often called a Costa Rican milkshake. It can be made with either water or milk, although some people don't consider it a batido without milk. It will be freshly run through a mixer with ice, fruit, and maybe sugar. Not all sodas have the blender power to offer batidos. Some fancier places now make smoothies with yogurt, ice cream, etc.

Traditional Costa Rican coffee is *chorreado*, poured. Ground coffee is put into an open cloth bag hung on a wooden or metal frame. Boiling water is poured through the coffee and collected in a container below. The procedure can be repeated until the coffee is sufficiently strong. This technique makes a very good cup of coffee. Electric coffee makers are increasingly common.

You can ask for *café negro*, black coffee, or *café con leche*, coffee with hot milk added. You will always be offered plenty of sugar. Coffee may or may not be included in the price of your breakfast. If you are offered *crema* for your coffee, it is not cream. It is non-dairy creamer.

Additionally, you can almost always order commercial carbonated soft drinks (*gaseosas*), bottled tea, energy drinks, beer, etc. Hot tea is less common, but often available if you ask.

CONDIMENTS

Mayonnaise and ketchup are universally offered and used, liberally, on almost everything. Two things to remember: the yellow squeeze bottle is mayo, not mustard; Costa Rican ketchup is much sweeter than the U.S. version. Tabasco sauce and *chilero* (generic Costa Rican hot sauce in a bottle) are usually available as well. Salsa Lizano is a ubiquitous table sauce that is made from "natural spices and vegetables" according to a secret family recipe. Lizano is a little sweet and sometimes compared to Worcestershire, which is sometimes offered as *salsa inglesa*. You will generally have to request salt or pepper.

Chilera (don't confuse this with chilero, bottled hot sauce) is a delight most foreigners pass on. This is a homemade concoction of chopped hot peppers, carrots, cauliflower, onions, shredded cabbage, green beans, and sweet peppers that have been pickled in vinegar for several weeks. Don't let an unattractive well-used container put you off this treat. Use the spoon in the jar to scoop out some chunks of spicy vegetables and pile them onto your plate. Every restaurant and bar has its own recipe for chilera and even that may vary with the availability of good produce.

Glossary of Food Terms

Ajillo – Cooked with garlic
Ajo - Garlic
Aros – Rings, circles
Aros de Calamar – Squid rings
Aros de Cebolla – Onion rings
Arracache – Starchy root
Arroz – Rice
Arroz con pollo – Rice with chicken
Azúcar - Sugar
Batido – Liquified fruit drink with ice
Banano – Banana
Boca – A small snack dish, like a Spanish tapa
Burrito – Burrito, deep fried in Costa Rica
Café – Coffee
Café Chorreado – Coffee poured through a hanging cloth bag
Café con Leche – Coffee with milk
Café Expreso - Espresso
Café Instantáneo – Instant coffee
Café Negro – Black coffee
Calamar – Squid
Caldo – Soup
Caldo de Pollo – Chicken soup
Cantonés (Arroz) – Cantonese rice dish
Camarón – Shrimp
Camarón del Río – Crayfish
Cas – Cas, a sour fruit used in refrescos
Carne – Meat
Casado – A big plate with different foods
Cebolla – Onion

Cerdo – Pig, pork

Cerveza – Beer

Ceviche – Ceviche, a word now in English as well

Chalupa – A toasted tortilla with toppings

Chicharrón – In Costa Rica, usually fried bits of pork

Chicharrón Crocante – Crispy pork rind

Chicharrón de Pellejo – Crispy pork rind

Chifrijo – A rice, bean, chicharrón, and chimichurri dish

Chilera – Homemade pickled hot peppers and vegetables

Chile - A pepper

Chile Dulce - A sweet pepper

Chile Panameño – A common red chile pepper, very hot

Chile Picante – Hot pepper

Chilero – Commercial hot sauce in a bottle

Chimichurri – Chopped tomatoes with onion, lime, and cilantro; pico de gallo

Chorizo – A small spicy sausage

Crema – Non-dairy powder for coffee; milk based soup

Cubierto – A setting of silverware

Culantro – Cilantro, Costa Rica uses the hard "cu" pronunciation

Culantro Coyote – An herb with long flat leaves and a cilantro taste

Encebollado – With onions

Enyucado – A snack made with cassava flour and a little meat inside

Empanada – A filled pastry, baked or fried

Fresa – Strawberry

Fresco – Fruit and water drink

Frijol – Bean

Frijol tierno – A common red bean

Frijoles Molidos – Refried beans

Gallina – Hen

Gallo – Rooster; soft tortilla with filling

Gallo pinto – Rice and beans

Guaro – Alcohol in general; clear inexpensive liquor

Hamburguesa - Hamburger

Helado – Ice cream

Hongo - Mushroom

Huevo – Egg

Huevos Fritos – Fried eggs

Huevos Fritos Tiernos – Fried eggs, lightly cooked

Huevos Fritos Bien Cocidos – Well cooked fried eggs

Huevos Revueltos – Scrambled eggs

Huevos Revueltos con tomate/jamón – Scrambled eggs with tomato/ham

Lechuga – Lettuce

Lengua - Tongue

Mariscos – Seafood in general

Masa – Corn dough

Mayonesa – Mayonaise

Mixto – Mixed

Mora - Rasberry

Morcilla – Blood sausage

Natilla – Liquid sour cream

Ñampí – A starchy root vegetable

Olla de Carne – A hearty soup-stew

Pan – Bread

Pan Cuadrado – Commercial white bread

Papa – Potato

Papas fritas – French fries

Papaya – Papaya

Parrilla - Grill

Patí – A fried pastry envelope with a meat stuffing

Pescado – Fish, caught for consumption

Pescado entero – Whole fish

Pez – Fish, uncaught

Piangua – A clam used in ceviche

Picadillo – A mild dish of diced potatoes and other vegetables

Picante – Spicy hot

Pinto – Short for gallo pinto

Plátano – Plantain

Plato – Plate

Plato fuerte – Main dish

Pollo – Chicken

Pollo Frito – Fried chicken

Piña – Pineapple; a pair of tamales tied together

Prensada – Fried sandwich between two tortillas, often with cheese

Pulpo – Octopus

Queso - Cheese

Refresco – Fruit and water drink

Repollo – Cabbage

Res – Beef

Sal – Salt

Salado – Salted; not sweet

Salchichón – A mild red sausage

Salsa de Carne – Meat sauce

Salsa de tomate – Ketchup

Salsa inglesa – Worcestershire sauce

Salsa picante – Hot sauce

Salsas – Mayo and ketchup; sauces

Sangrita – Spicy tomato juice

Servilleta – Napkin

Sopa – Soup

Sopa Azteca – A tomato soup

Sopa de Mariscos – Seafood soup

Sopa Negra – Black bean soup

Sustancia – Broth of beef, chicken or fish

Taco – Taco, fried in Costa Rica

Tiquisque – A starchy root
Tomate - Tomato
Tortilla de Maíz – Corn tortilla
Tortilla de Trigo – Wheat flour tortilla
Tortilla Aliñada – A tortilla with cheese mixed into the dough
Tostada - Toast
Tierno – Soft
Vaso – Glass
Vaso con hielo – Glass with ice
Vino – Wine
Vino Blanco – White wine
Vino Tinto – Red wine
Vigorón – A dish with chicharrón crocante, cassava, and cabbage salad
Yuca - Cassava

Bibliography

Arauz Ramos, Carlos Enrique. *Costa Rica, leyendas y tradiciones.* San José,

Costa Rica: Impresiones Dinámicas, 2010.

Arauz Ramos, Carlos Enrique. *Guanacaste, Life and Culture.* Translation:

Adriana Quirós and Susana Arauz. San José, Costa Rica, 2006.

Cabal Antillón, Dionisio. *Los Agüizotes: Raíces mágicas de Costarrica.* San José,

Costa Rica: Cultura Producciones, 2009.

Costa Rica. Ministerio de Cultura y Juventud and Centro de Conervación

Patrimonio Cultural. *La cuchara de la Abuela.* San José, Costa Rica: Sabores, 2012.

Mitchell, Meg Tyler and Pintzer, Scott. *COSTA RICA: A Global Studies*

Handbook. Santa Barbara, CA: ABC-CLIO, 2008.

Padilla, María Mayela. *Leyendas de Tiquicia.* San José, Costa Rica: Guilá, 2011.

Jack Donnelly

Palmer, Steven and Molina, Iván, eds. *THE COSTA RICA READER: History,*

Culture, Politics. Durham and London: Duke, 2004

Sandy. *Comidas a la Tica*. San José, Costa Rica, 2012.

Sandy. *Leyendas a la Tica*. San José, Costa Rica, 2008.

Sandy. *"Para siempre. Tradiciones Ticas." Volumen 1*. San José, Costa Rica,

2008.

Sandy. *Refranes y Adivinazas de mi tierra*. San José, Costa Rica, 2008.

Sierra Quinteno, Oscar, and "RODICAB", Ronald Díaz. LEYENDAS

costarricenses en Novela Gráfica. San José, Costa Rica: la pluma comic, 2011.

Zeledón, Elías. *LEYENDAS COSTARRICENSES*. Comp. Heredia, Costa Rica:

EUNA, 2011.

Jack Donnelly has been a life-long enthusiast of Latin American folk culture. As a young man, during the 1960s, he studied cultural anthropology at the Universidad de las Américas in Mexico City. He went on to volunteer with the Peace Corps in Guatemala, working with Mayan cooperatives in the Western Highlands and adding to his knowledge and appreciation of Central America's rich cultural heritage.

Spending much of his adult life in New Hampshire, Donnelly had to work hard to maintain his Spanish and fuel his interest in Spanish-speaking culture. Over the years, he has published multiple articles and photographs on Costa Rica.

Now, Donnelly lives in Heredia, Costa Rica. He travels around the country investigating and documenting folkloric events. His book *Costa Rica* gathers his findings into a culture-rich guide that offers unique insight into the traditions of the country.

14014463R00069

Made in the USA
San Bernardino, CA
12 August 2014